A MOST
BEAUTIFUL
THING

A MOST BEAUTIFUL THING

*The True Story of America's First
All-Black High School Rowing Team*

ARSHAY COOPER

FLATIRON
BOOKS
NEW YORK

This is a true story, but some names and details have been changed.

www.flatironbooks.com

The Library of Congress Cataloging-in-Publication Data is available upon request.

ISBN 978-1-250-75476-9 (hardcover)
ISBN 978-1-250-75475-2 (ebook)

Our books may be purchased in bulk for promotional,
educational, or business use. Please contact your local bookseller or
the Macmillan Corporate and Premium Sales Department at 1-800-221-7945,
extension 5442, or by email at MacmillanSpecialMarkets@macmillan.com.

Originally published in 2015 under the title
Suga Water by Wise Ink Creative Publishing

First Flatiron Books Edition: 2020

10 9 8 7 6 5 4 3 2 1

TO STACY AND SASHA,

TO MY MOTHER, WHO REPRESENTS HOPE,

AND TO THE CITY OF CHICAGO, WHO'S IN SEARCH OF IT

Contents

We take off. I'm in the two-seat rowing port, and I can feel the spray of the stroke seat blade splashing water back at me. "Balance the boat!" I yell. We find our timing and hit 200 meters. We settle in, driving hard and recovering. Driving and recovering. We reach 600 meters, and I feel the boat slow. My pulse quickens. "We're halfway there! Keep pushing! You have been through much harder than this!" Coach screams. I kick up the gears even though my body is ready to give in. But when you no longer can row with your legs, you must row with your heart. Now 200 to go. "Lighten fast," Coach calls. My mind starts playing tricks on me, saying shit like you're not built for balancing boats, callused hands, open water, and regattas—that I don't belong in this ancient sport so long reserved for schools like Harvard and Yale, Oxford and Cambridge. Places light-years away from the West Side of Chicago. In this moment, I am in a game of tug-of-war between the me in the boat and the me the world expects. But I am not the only one fighting here. My muscles surge with adrenaline as my team pushes forward in unison.

I

Holy City

Growing up, we had a fan in our apartment that made a loud clicking noise. We couldn't afford a new one so we kept it. After a while, the clicking noise didn't bother us, almost like it wasn't there. We only remembered when new people visited and reminded us of the noise. That's how the violence in our city was during the summer.

I came from the West Side. At fourteen years old in my neighborhood, kids had experienced what most soldiers witnessed in war. At fifteen, I had already run for my life, had bullets fly straight past my head, skipped over pools of blood, and witnessed dead bodies on the street. On my block, there were eleven raggedy-ass buildings, five vacant lots filled with empty forty-ounce beer bottles, and four liquor stores that lock down each corner. It's hard to believe in the American Dream when you walk home through streets of abandoned buildings scattered with baggies of drugs. It was like God existed everywhere but here.

The rules of each street were set by different gangs. If I wore certain colors in the wrong neighborhood, I could get shot. If I wore my baseball cap slightly to the left or to the right in the wrong neighborhood, I could get shot. If I scratched my head and it looked like my fingers were making a certain gesture in the wrong neighborhood, I could get shot. I couldn't even wear Converse shoes in some neighborhoods because the star symbol is a five-point star, and the five-point star represented the Almighty Vice Lord Nation.

My neighborhood was called "Holy City" because every gang in it ends with the word Lord. There were Conservative Vice Lords, Traveling Vice Lords, Insane Vice Lords, Renegade Vice Lords, and Unknown Vice Lords. When the guys saw one another they said, "What up, Lord?" In Holy City, there were also zombies in every direction. That's what I called the drug addicts. My mother used to be one of them. My aunts and uncles were, too. Their arms were the first thing I'd notice, always clawing for something. Their eyes had no soul, like the life had been sucked out of them. They were as thin as drinking straws and spoke no words, only noises. They were in the hallways of my building, and I was petrified every time I tiptoed past them through the cloud of rock cocaine.

There were no pictures of me from before the age of thirteen; drugs took them. There were no memories of kisses good night or the smell of breakfast in the morning; rock cocaine's to blame. There were no good grades, no junior high sweethearts, no ability to be popular at school, and no sense of belonging, thanks to alcohol abuse. These were not my addictions, but my mother's, and bitterness was stamped on the tablet of my heart.

Back when I was thirteen, I did something I regret. I chose to believe my mom was dead. I had a funeral in my heart. I knew she was going to die in the streets. She was losing so much weight, she stole our Christmas gifts, and she would only come home two or three days a week. When she came home, she would cry aloud in the middle of the night and scream for her fix. I didn't know who she was anymore. She would dress herself in so many layers, one on top of the other, and when I saw her in the streets she was always with a different guy.

I counted her out. I didn't respect her and treated her like a dead woman roaming the streets. I didn't really know my biological father and figured he left my mom for the same reason I wanted to leave, so I was bitter and blamed her. I have heard of other parents in our neighborhood dying from overdoses and my mom seemed far worse than they'd been. I wanted to prepare myself mentally and emotionally for when my mother left us because of drugs, so I could be strong for my brothers and sisters. I reached inside and decided she was already gone. It was the same feeling you get when the police or state troopers are behind you and it's only a matter of time before they stop you. I stopped thinking about her, I stopped worrying about her, but I still cried because I loved her too much and knew she couldn't stop. She had four kids she loved, so she would stop if she could, right? She was all I ever wanted and needed, but I felt like I had to be strong at thirteen. I would stay up at night waiting for her to come home with her usual hysterics, just so I could fall asleep afterward.

A week passed with no sign of her. Two weeks, no mom. I was annoyed because she had gotten a check and was supposed to buy us clothes. Three weeks, no sign, and I thought to myself that maybe she was gone. I was worried, but not upset. It was as though my heart went cold. We were all living with my grandmother at the time, and after a month passed, there was finally a call. My grandmother said that my mother had checked into a rehab home called Victory Outreach Christian Recovery Homes and wanted us to visit. I figured it wouldn't last. Six months passed. My brothers and sister would visit, but I never did; I didn't want to see her. She was dead to me.

A month later, my grandmother forced me to go to a Victory Outreach service to visit my mom. My mother was sweating her to make sure I came. The church was on the corner of Twenty-sixth Street and South Karlov Avenue, a tumultuous Mexican neighborhood. The Two-Six gang was hanging on the corner and I thought to myself, "Will I survive this night?" If you are black and live on the West Side of Chicago you know you do not cross the viaduct into the Mexican neighborhood. This is where the police drop you off when you mouth off to them and try to be a tough guy; it's like being dropped in the middle of the ocean.

When we entered the building there was beautiful music, different from anything I had ever heard. There were pictures of people of different ethnicities along the wall leading up the stairs. There was a black man and a white woman at the front door to the sanctuary, greeting me with a big smile. When I entered, everyone had their hands lifted. There were blacks, whites, Mexicans, Puerto Ricans. Young people and old, and they all looked at peace. I had never witnessed such a thing. There was ocean-blue furniture, bright white walls, and fresh flowers everywhere. The instruments were polished to a shine and the smell was invigorating. This was not a service but an experience.

I looked toward the stage and saw my mother up there singing. I was in shock. Her eyes were watering and her face was glowing, and she beamed when she saw me. When I smiled back something churned inside and I thought, *She's alive.* She was beautiful, devilishly beautiful, and she had joy like a river in her soul. After the songs, a man went onstage, grabbed the microphone, and spoke to us.

"Happy Thanksgiving and welcome to Victory Outreach Church. Take your seat. You are going to hear some live testimonies from people that were once not people." I wondered what that meant.

"Sister Linda Cooper, come to the mic!" he shouted. My heart started pounding. I felt a little embarrassed, hoping she didn't point me out. Very softly and slowly, her hands shaking, she said, "Hey, my name is Sister Linda Cooper. I am a mother of four and my kids are here today."

Everyone started clapping. She went on, "I want to thank God for my salvation, because I was supposed to be dead in some alley by now. I can't believe I didn't lose my mind from all the drugs. I mean, every drug you name, I done it and I was addicted to it."

She started crying and people shouted to encourage her. "Come on now, you got this!"

She continued, "I was all messed up, I was a cheater, and I stole from my kids. I didn't know how to love my kids. I was angry, I hated my life, and so I made a decision after I spent all my kids' money that I was going to kill myself. I mean, I was sitting there with rock cocaine in a TV antenna, smoking it. I couldn't look my kids in their eyes anymore. I was walking down the street with my head down on my way to end my life, and then a guy handed me a flyer and said 'Jesus loves you.' When I looked back, he was gone.

"I walked to this woman's house to call this place on the flyer, her name was Ms. Stella. She was an old wise lady in the neighborhood who helped me out from time to time. We called the Victory Outreach program, and they said they were full. Ms. Stella wouldn't let me leave her house. She said, 'If you go back out there, don't ever speak to me again.' I stayed there in bed for three days until I got a call from Victory Outreach. They said there was room.

"So, I got up and left and walked and walked. It was so far, it had to be miles. I had no money, my feet were hurting, but I felt something pushing me towards the Victory Outreach home. I wanted to turn around but I couldn't. Something was pushing me. Ever since that day, seven months ago, I been clean, I been changed, I have hope and a future, and there is no looking back."

I was clapping; I didn't cry, but I wanted to. At that moment, I decided to try to let it go, all the hatred I had toward her, the pain, the memories of kids at school making my life hell because of her addiction, the sleepless, hungry nights. In my heart, I had forgiven her before she opened her mouth. I didn't want to, because that year had seen my darkest hours and my deepest depression. But I knew when she came home, I had to be patient with her, love her, laugh with her, talk with her, pray with her, walk with her, and try to get to know her.

After the service, my mother sat with us and had dinner downstairs in the church fellowship hall. My mother told us that her father was a very violent man—that he beat and raped her and that she often felt it was her responsibility to keep her two younger sisters safe. I kept staring at this woman, my mother, staring right into her eyes and I could see all her hurt and feel all her feelings. I wanted to hug her, but we were not an affectionate family. But as she was telling us she looked so different, she even sounded different.

I had known my grandfather was a violent man. When I was nine years old, he pushed through the door drunkenly, yelling, "I am the war lord! I am the G!" He was a very big man. My grandmother came into the kitchen in her nightgown telling him to calm down and cut the noise out. He grabbed her and tried to rip her gown off as he dropped his pants to force himself on her. My grandmother was screaming, so my brother Shaundell jumped on my grandfather's back and I started pushing him off her as she was hitting him upside the head with a boot. My grandmother pushed him toward the stove, which had all the burners lit—it was how we got heat. I saw my grandfather put his hand onto the grate, directly over the flame. I got scared, so I tried to pull him off but I couldn't move his arm. I didn't scream but I do remember thinking to myself that even though my grandfather was a bad man, *I saved his life*. I also felt like I was cursed with weakness, because he deserved to burn.

Remembering that incident alone, I can only imagine what my mother went through.

I never believed in God because of my situation and my environment. I was always very confused about this God. Growing up, I saw people shot and killed, and I heard their families say there was no God if all their babies were dying. Then there were those who would get hit and survive, and say it was only God who spared their life. I was indeed confused. That day, I wondered what it was that saved my mother. I was interested to find out.

Hearing the testimonies, I learned that Victory Outreach was a Christian-based but nondenominational church that could be found in nearly every inner city in the world. I heard the pastor say that their mission was to reach the drug addicts, the gang members, the prostitutes, and the brokenhearted. Even the "Goody Two-shoes" who have never broken a plate in their lives.

"What we have in common is that we are suffering from a void," he said, "so we look for love in all the wrong places. We try money, drugs, sex, fame, parties. And because of that we end up crying out for help. That's where Victory Outreach steps in. We offer a home for men and women. We have youth programs, church services, sports programs, workshops. See, we are not just some other program, some social agency, or some little church on the corner. Some of our people tried AA, tried psychiatrists, doctors, gang programs, jail, and nothing worked. It wasn't religion but a spiritual relationship with God that changed us.

"It's like a big watermelon, I can take it and split it open and eat it and tell you it tastes good, it's so juicy, but until you try it yourself you will never know. God called us out of the ghettos to go back to the ghettos and make a difference. We are called to reach the treasures out of darkness, people who were once not people, but are now beautiful people of God."

In that moment I thought *God, if you're there, open my eyes and heart to see that this is for real.*

At 6:00 a.m. my alarm goes off. I jump up quickly, as if from a bad dream.

It's the fall of 1997 in Chicago. The city is still vibrant after the Bulls won their fifth championship this past summer. When the trophy is home, every Chicagoan jumps on the L train downtown straight to Grant Park wearing the number 23. While Richard Daley is the mayor of the city, I feel like it should be Michael Jordan. The celebration rally brings together a diverse group of people in ways local leaders have not. On that day, there are no differences. You get to experience all that Chicago has to offer, from stuffed pizza to the Magnificent Mile. When that day is over, you're back in your community with people who look like you, separated from other communities by viaducts.

I live in this dingy one-bedroom apartment with my two brothers, Isaac and Shaundell; my little sister, Pamela; and now my God-fearing mother, Linda. I still don't know why my mom named me Arshay, but I love that it's unique. I am the middle child between the oldest, Shaudell, and Isaac, the youngest. My mom and Pamela share the sofa bed in the front room, and my brothers and I share the bedroom. We have an old bunk bed from the thrift store that Shaundell and Isaac sleep on and I have the mattress on the floor. That's what happens when you are the middle child. There is only one TV in the apartment, and it sits on an old wooden chair. Most fights at home start over whose turn it is to watch their favorite show, but when that happens, my mom always changes it to TBN, the Christian network. Those old white men preaching have the opposite effect and scare the Jesus *out* of me. We don't have much at home besides this TV, a wooden chair, kitchen table, bunk bed, and mattress, but we have each other.

My little sister is the prettiest little doll I know. She has thin Twizzler-like braids and she wears colorful berets. At twelve years old, she is very mouthy and we joke that she swallowed a radio. Isaac is just one year older than Pamela, and he is an asshole to the tenth power. I wring his neck at least once a day. He is short and bulky. It is my belief that he is the cause of a few teachers deciding to make a career change. Isaac wants to be like Shaundell. Shaundell is one of the cool kids. He is slender, and the ladies love his dimples. He is sweet-tempered and always finds a way to buy Mom gifts. I am not sure how he gets the money, but I'm afraid that we are losing him to the streets. He comes home late smelling like Mary Jane, and the guys he rolls with are gang members. My mom prays daily for Shaundell. So do I. In the Cooper household, we are always loyal to family.

As I lie in bed, I hear my mom shout, "Time to get up and pray!"

She is clapping her hands and singing.

He that believeth, he that believeth have an everlasting life.

He that believeth in the Father and the Son have an everlasting life.
When I get to heaven I'm gonna walk all around, have an everlasting
  life.
When I get to heaven, I'm gonna put on my crown, have everlasting
  life.

Isaac complains about having to wake up so early to this noise.

"As for me and my house, we serve the Lord," my mother responds. Shaundell is quiet, his head down, not saying a word.

Morning devotion is a daily routine in our apartment Monday through Sunday. We wake up to my mom's songs, we complain a little, and then we fight to get into the bathroom. We each have to find a scripture to read out loud, we sing a song (usually "Amazing Grace" or "God Will Make a Way"), and my mother asks if we have a prayer request. Afterward, we get on our knees and pray for a half hour. Most of the time we just fall back to sleep, but if we get caught sleeping, we have to stand the whole time. The weird thing is that sometimes my siblings will pray, sometimes they won't, but you can always tell one from the other. The sibling who prays always feels good afterward and minds their own business. Mother asks of us daily to pray for Ike, who she married many years ago. He is the father of Isaac and Pamela. Right now, he is a captive bird in the state penitentiary for selling drugs. Ike always said, "There are no rules when it comes to survival and feeding your family." I felt like the money was feeding his drug habit. Mom was always intrigued by his edginess, I think. Secretly, I hope he stays in. Mom needs no harmful influences. So that's my prayer.

We head in different directions to school. My younger brother Isaac and little sister Pamela are at Mason Elementary School, Shaundell is a junior at Farragut Career Academy, and I attend Manley Career Academy as a sophomore. Manley is known for its success in basketball, but we also have a rep for being one of the most violent schools on the West Side. At the time, Manley graduated less than 60 percent of its senior class every year and only sent 10 percent of its senior class to college. A day at Manley starts with waiting in a ridiculously long line to walk through the metal detectors. I get that it keeps us safe, but no one can get to class on time. I've seen security guards confiscate wrenches, pocket knives, screwdrivers, and even box cutters. Most of these weapons are generally for protection after school. There are school security guards on each floor of the building to protect the 600 kids that go to school here. All these kids are African American and, for the most part, love being Wildcats. Everyone refers to one another as *joe*. In California, they say "What's up, homes"; in New York, it's "What's up, son"; and we say "What's up, joe." At Manley, you have to bring it when it comes to the clothes you sport. All the cool kids wear Levi's, Echo, COOGI, and Phat Farm. When it comes to kicks, they better be Nikes, Air Jordans, Adidas, or Timberlands if you want to be spotted by the ladies. I am wearing Filas and Lee jeans, which means another year of being the invisible man.

Manley has decent basketball, football, and baseball teams for boys and the girls have volleyball and basketball. To make these teams, you have to be incredibly gifted. You have about 400 students trying out for these programs and only about 150 of them making it. That leaves 250 people just chilling between afterschool and six o'clock, which is prime time for risky behavior like sexing it up, getting jumped into a gang, fights, and horseplay. Public school is tough for teachers, too. In our classes, there are at least thirty students; sometimes one class has members of three or four separate gangs. Our teachers spend a lot of time breaking up fights. Good teachers are creative enough to keep us interested in our subjects so there is no room to think about the guy on the other side of the classroom. I realize that it's tough; some of these gangs are even separated from each other in prison. The teachers have to be peacemakers, mentors, parents, friends, security guards, and social workers. It's stressing them out; I notice it when I see them leaving the restroom or teacher's lounge in tears.

I take the city bus to school. The L train is faster, but I have to walk through three different gang territories to get there, and I don't feel like being chased today. Every so often, when I'm late for school, I will haul ass down Pulaski Road to the L train. My bus rides are usually the same: loud. When I get on the bus, it's crammed with students from four different high schools. I call it "the pickle jar." Half the time when a fight breaks out the bus driver keeps rolling. They make it known that they don't get paid enough to break up fights. When I get off the bus on Sacramento Street, just a few blocks from the school, there is always the risk of being greeted with a beating by the Travelers Vice Lords. The city of Chicago has about fifty different gangs and hundreds of different cliques—splinter groups. Some are known for their fancy cars, and others are notable for being stone-cold killers. These guys were born into this village, and this is all they know. I don't think these guys join because they believe it's going to be a good time, but for protection from the gang on the next block over and to be a part of something.

I steer clear of the Travelers Vice Lords and find my way to first period. What I do like about Manley is the five career-preparation schools within the school, which are trade schools. They are Medical Arts, Graphics & Technology, Construction, Business, and Foods & Hospitality. I want to be a chef.

First period is home ec, and everyone is tasked with cooking omelets. Instead I quietly work on a poem, trying not to think about home. As I'm writing my masterpiece, I hear footsteps behind me. Nisha—a tall, skinny, very loud, and obnoxious girl—walks over and dumps a handful of salt on top of my head and shouts, "Get up and cook, nigga!" Without thinking, I jump up and force my forearm in her neck. She starts punching me on the top of my head. With my forearm pressure on her neck, I stop and stare in her eyes and ask what her problem is. I realize that I'm freaking out and let her go. I know, and she knows, that I am a kind kid, and not in a million years would I usually react like that. She is just being her normal, obnoxious self. Nisha is certified hood. She is responsible for most of our classroom laughs. Chef Singleton, our instructor, tells us both to take a seat and he doesn't report us to the office. Chef Singleton likes me a lot, and knows I have what it takes to be great, but he knows I'm always in my head.

We sit down and everyone is quiet. I can feel Nisha looking at me with tears in her eyes, still in shock. I never look back up. I feel really bad—I've never done something like this before. Some of the class is happy and thinks Nisha got what she deserves. I am ashamed. I go back to writing; I only have a couple sentences so far.

> *Sometimes I wonder, sometimes I think,*
> *As I am lying in my bed, hopeless, will the sailboat really sink?*
> *What I mean is, like the great big Titanic,*
> *As the boat was sinking, people love to start to panic.*
> *I don't have the looks or the charm or the smarts*
> *But what I do have is a huge, pure, undivided heart.*
> *I don't have skills that are recognizable by all,*
> *To some, I am probably a shepherd boy, waiting on God's call.*

I write this poem for the one and only Grace, the smartest girl in our sophomore class. She has half-inch dimples, a perfectly round head, and neck-length, natural black hair. Plus, she looks so good in purple. Her eyes are brown and shine like diamonds. I love to hear her talk in the hallways. Her voice carries a Southern lilt, loud and sweet, that echoes through concrete. Her body isn't important to me, but she does have a heavenly one—she is a cheerleader and one of those girls you will only find in an episode of *The Fresh Prince of Bel-Air*. Grace seems easy like Sunday morning while the other girls seem hard to deal with like Monday morning.

Freshman year, she chose Derrick. Handsome, swagged-out, tall, in-shape, basketball-playing Derrick. He appears to be flawless, an affable scholar-athlete; he ranks number one in our class. If you made a movie of our class, Derrick and Grace are the ones who would be the stars. I have heard through the grapevine that they are broken up and she is not taking it well. This is good and bad news because for some reason I feel like I am the one that can open up her heart. Guys like Derrick get the girl that everyone wants and forget that they're still the girl everyone wants. It's been a long time coming, but the problem is we never speak; I don't even think she knows I exist.

The bell rings and I storm out of class. My pride won't allow me to apologize to Nisha. I am just glad to have favor with Chef Singleton. I walk into the hall to the smell of hair grease and Flamin' Hot Cheetos and hear "Cooper!" Preston saunters in my direction wearing a fresh pair of Air Force 1s and some slick black Levi's.

I'm a bit of a loner, but Preston is my best friend. We've been in the same school since fifth grade. He's a tall, skinny kid with slim eyes and short hair with amazing waves. He is by far the smoothest and most confident kid I know, and the ladies love him. Preston gets his swag from his mother, who is considered the coolest mom in our neighborhood. Her name is Michelle, and she has sold weed for the longest of anyone I know. I never judge because she plays no games when it comes to raising her children. She makes sure that her kids' grades are good, and if their grades aren't good, they are punished. Michelle always welcomes me in her home with open arms and feeds me when I have a terrible day. I have never told her what's going on, she just knows, I guess. *A mother always knows.*

"What's up, Coop?" he asks as he catches up to me.

"Nothing, man, I had a bad night at home and now a lousy day at school," I say with my head dropped down to the floor.

Preston lightly punches me in the chest, says "Motivation," and walks away.

I spend the whole day at school waiting for it to be over, but when the final bell rings and I walk outside, I'm met with a crowd in the street of about ten guys walking toward someone. The lone guy is yelling, "Four Corner Hustlers!" At the front of the group is the same pretty boy who eyed me down in the hallway with the ladies.

I see him throw an orange at the one kid, and when the kid's hands go up to block it they all rush him. One of them hits him with a right cross, and he falls hard. The crowd is getting big. They start stomping him. One guy picks him up so that they can hit him some more, and I can see his blood flying with his spit. Girls are yelling out, "You killing him, you killing him!" And they drop him to the ground. They beat him until he's shaking and his eyes are rolling back in his head. Then a guy with a box haircut gets out of a car, pulls out a gun, and asks, "Do I need to use this?" The group says no and they all run.

These boys are called the Straight Off Albany Clique (S.O.A. for short). They are the biggest gang in school and are connected to the Traveling Vice Lords. I've witnessed the S.O.A. beat people into seizures more than once. I've also seen these guys take bags full of piss, tie them into knots, and toss them into crowds. No one will confront them. During separate days in the month of October, fifty or sixty of them threw eggs into the afterschool crowds. One day, all the security guards from the school were fed up, and fifteen of them marched toward the gang with their white shirts on. It seemed like the security guards were about to do some damage until one of the kids gave the signal and eggs went flying in from everywhere, hitting the guards until they ran back into the school.

There is no stopping these guys; they do what they want when they want. This isn't new to me at all. I duck out of the action and head home. I feel like I've seen worse.

2

Barbershop Prayers

Its lunchtime the following day and I can hear the yelling from three staircases up. I walk in and see this long, thin, snazzy white boat. Behind it is an old shitty television monitor showing people racing in the same boat. I stand there, dumbstruck. I have never seen anything like this before.

Someone taps me on the shoulder. "Hey, I am Coach Jessica. Would you like to be on the crew team?" Living on the West Side, my body tenses and gets ready to run at the mention of a *crew*, but I turn around and am met with the smiling face of a white lady.

"What's that?" I say.

"It's rowing, come and let me show you on the TV," she says gleefully. I glance around to see who is looking. Kids are giggling and all the fellas are staring at her booty and shaking each other's hands. Coach Jessica's hair falls straight and looks like an Amish corn whisk broom. Her skin is both pale and red, like a white-fleshed peach. She is rocking some faded blue jeans and a white T-shirt that is basically beige. I walk over to the TV and look closer and see nothing but white people.

"Oh no," I whisper and walk away.

"Hey, young man!" she shouts. I just keep it moving to the snack station to buy a soda. Splitting like that is rude and insensitive, but white-people shit like that gets you killed. In front of me is the same pretty boy who jumped that guy yesterday.

"Can I get a super donut!" he shouts at the lunch lady. She's this sassy old grump who rolls her eyes each time a student orders something. When she turns around to get the donut, he reaches over to steal chips and tosses them to his friends. When she turns back around, he says, "It's okay. I don't have my money." I guess he is the Manley Wildcats' Robin Hood. He walks away and sits with the S.O.A. crew.

I pay for my soda and sit down at the table with Preston.

The only ones at our table are us two and Dirty Herb. His real name is Joe, but he's called Dirty Herb because he smells like a marijuana dispensary. I don't know much more about him than that. I never chat it up with him.

"Whatsup, joe," Preston says.

"Nothin' man, you see those crazy white folks with the boat?"

"Yeah Coop, this is how the white people kill us off," Preston utters humorlessly.

"I'm not saying all that, but you ain't gonna get black people rowing down the lake like slaves."

Preston grabs his stale-looking slice of pizza, points it to me and says, "Think about it, joe, even the boat is white." A roar of laughter comes from Dirty Herb. I laugh, too.

"All jokes aside, what are you doing after school?" I say.

"Chillin'; come by the crib. My mom will love to see you."

I give Preston a fist bump. "I'll think about it."

"Cool."

I glance back at the boat over my shoulder. *Good luck.*

At four o'clock, I find myself sitting on Preston's front porch with a couple of homies from the block. Preston lives in a single-family home that is old as dirt. The porch used to be white, but now it's brown because all of the paint peeled off. Two guys from the Conservative Vice Lord gang are chilling with us. Kenny and Randy both come from a family of gang-bangers, but they're cool with me because we grew up together.

Randy taps my shoulder and says, "Heads up."

I look up and see Preston's older sister's best friend, Big T. My heart drops. Big T has been bullying me since I was thirteen. He's five years older and is tall and built like a linebacker. His clothes are always name brand from head to toe, and he has a strong voice. When he speaks, people just shut up and listen.

At some point, Big T. developed a strong passion for making my life a living hell. One time when I was hanging out with all of my buddies and the girls from the neighborhood, Big T. showed up looking for Tiana, Preston's sister. When he saw me he gathered the whole crowd together to talk shit about my mom. I hate this guy.

Big T. walks up on the porch and looks directly at me. "Everyone look at Arshay; he had these clothes on yesterday and the day before. What are you, a cartoon character?" Only Kenny laughs.

"Chill out," Preston says to him.

Big T. lifts my arm. "Everyone smell this. His damn crackhead mother can't even afford deodorant for him. Look at his old Filas."

I want to crack him right in the jaw, but he is rock solid and probably has a metal chin. He looks me in my eye, and I stare back. This time I am not going to cry. I may have smelled then, but I know I don't now.

He keeps going. "Why do you even exist? Why is your mom a junkie? Dude, go home and shower, you should be ashamed of yourself." Anger bubbles up inside my chest and I feel my fingers flex, but right when I'm about to say something Preston grabs me.

"Come on, Coop, I will walk you to the bus stop."

Big T. shouts, "You better go."

"He is a straight jerk," Preston says to me as we walk down the block.

"It's all good, Preston; I got it from here, I can walk on my own."

"Okay, Coop. See you tomorrow, joe."

On the bus, I start to question myself. What did I do wrong for him to treat me like this? Do I really look and smell that bad? I don't seem to fit in anywhere. If any girls liked me when I was a kid, they wouldn't anymore after Big T. finished clowning me. He gives me a bad reputation in the neighborhood. Guys like this push you to sell drugs for money to buy better clothes. I don't want to be a loser, but I want something better than this shit place. It's a lonely ride home.

When I get to the lunchroom the next day, I notice the big white boats are still there. This time, there's a long line of students around them and the rowing people are saying, "Come to the gym room today to sign up and get free pizza." I figure no one showed up yesterday.

I sit down at the table next to Preston and joke, "These people don't get it. Black people don't know how to swim, and you going to place them in *Jaws* territory?"

"I was thinking maybe we should join."

I give Preston a look. "Hell no! I can't even swim."

"I can't swim either, but the lady said free pizza and that we'd even go out of town."

"Nope."

"Come on, dude, let's just get pizza and leave."

I think for a minute. There's no way in hell I'm getting into one of those boats without something in return. And then an idea comes to me. "If you hook me up with Grace I will go. I will even join the damn team."

He takes a deep breath and says, "I will hook you up with anyone else but her."

"No one else will do."

"I will introduce you two, then you take it from there."

I tell Preston he has to tell her I like her. "Listen, I can't sleep. I am writing poems about this girl, and when I am having the absolute worst day of my life, the thought of her gives me peace."

Preston looks at me funny and gives in. Maybe he still feels bad from yesterday but knows I don't want to talk about it.

Preston dated Grace's best friend for a while, so he knows her well. He's also a smooth talker. He doesn't seem happy about the arrangement, but I trust him when it comes to girls.

School ends, and I'm excited and nervous at the same time. I have been rehearsing what I'm going to say in my head all day. Well, honestly, I've been rehearsing all year. Preston and I are waiting by the stairs at the main entrance for her. Fifteen minutes pass, no Grace. Thirty minutes pass, no Grace.

Preston tries to talk me into still attending the rowing demonstration, but I'm going home. He tries to tell me we have a deal, but I tell him there is no deal if he doesn't introduce me to Grace.

"No Grace, no rowing."

Preston can tell I am going to be stubborn, and decides to go without me.

I head home, cursing Preston. My brother Isaac and I put on a scary movie. My mom comes in the front door asking if we've seen Shaundell. We shake our heads, not even looking up from the TV.

"Those movies aren't allowed in my house," she says.

"Why not, Mom?" Isaac asks.

"Because fear is not of God, and you're only watching for fear, to scare yourself. Why would you want to be scared? Be inspired."

I have no answer for that, so I tell her I will go read *To Kill a Mockingbird* for English class. I get through one page, close the book, and ask my mom if I can have ten dollars to go get a haircut. She gives it to me and I head to the barbershop.

The barbershop is the black man's country club. That's where I go when I'm bored. I figured it's better than hanging in the streets. My mom made it very clear that if you hang in the streets, you will have to leave the house. The barbershop sells everything: gym shoes, T.D. Jakes's preaching tapes, porn, weed, candles. You name it, they have it. Most of the time the crackheads come in trying to sell you stuff they stole from you.

I open the door and the bell clangs. My barber, Dee, looks up and smiles. I know he spent some time in prison, but I'm not sure what for. All I know is that he is one wise dude and always kicking knowledge to the young bucks in the shop. He is in his mid-thirties, short and beefy and can pass for a macho man.

"How is school, Arshay?" Dee says.

"It's cool. I want to try out for the basketball team, but I'm mad scared."

"Bruh, you have to be willing to do it afraid. I was scared when I cut hair for the first time, but I did it."

I slip into his chair. "I guess I am just distracted."

"Boy, don't let the small distractions destroy your journey. Just keep going forward. You will get there." Dee sends the chair around, and I look in the mirror and see that my sideburns are skinny at the top and thick at the bottom.

"Dee, you got me looking like Elvis with these sideburns."

"Look like who? Boy, Elvis is white!"

I laugh and move my hands around wildly. "Even it out."

An old man with gray hair sitting next to me pipes up, "Listen to me, young man. I went to Europe, and while I was there I saw somebody from the West Side of Chicago. He was blown away to see me. That man told me this really is a small world, but I told him he was wrong. I said, 'If you look at the map, it's huge. This is a big world we live in, but you and I chose to expand.'"

I nod. "Yes, sir."

When I get home, Shaundell is still not back and my mom is calling everyone. My cousin tells her the guys he is hanging out with are in a gang war with another gang. Why he tells her that, I don't know. She is worried. She tells us that maybe we should all get on our knees and pray. I get on my knees and just think about Grace the whole time. I figure he will be home later.

My brother is a Gangster Disciple. He joined the gang a long time ago when my mom was still on drugs. Now that she's out of the recovery home, he is struggling between hanging with the guys and working on our new life as a family. I have my struggles, too, but I always tell Shaundell that being out there is like dying for a neighborhood you don't even know. The homeboys tell you they got your back, but weeks later you're nothing but a memory. There is no way I am going to trade my life in for a spray-painted shirt, a 40-ounce, and an R.I.P. sign on the wall. I'm worth more, and I tell Shaundell he is, too. He even mentions joining the Victory Outreach Christian Recovery Home just to get away. He tells me he will join in his own time. Time runs out early for people like us on the West Side.

The next day after second period English class, I see Preston dancing toward me in the hallway. "Coop, you missed out, because rowing was pretty dope. They have these crazy rowing machines that will leave you looking like baby Arnold Schwarzenegger."

"I went to the shop."

"Nice cut, Coop," Preston says, admiring my head. "Oh! And Grace came to rowing tryouts yesterday."

"Fool, you lying!"

He gives me a sly grin. "Yeah, I'm lying, but the boats will be back in the gym today."

"One word: Grace."

He winks. "Chill out, I got you."

At the end of the day, I meet Preston downstairs by the front entrance again. He is telling me how the people from the old neighborhood miss me and are always asking how I am doing. I look up and see Grace walking out the back entrance near the teachers' parking lot. I grab Preston.

"Dude, there she is, go get her!"

I follow behind him as the door closes behind her. He opens the door and calls out. I am nervous and shut the door behind him and start pacing back and forth in the hallway. Three minutes pass and I am freaking out and talking to myself. After what feels like a hundred years, Preston opens the door and shouts out to me.

"Coop, get out here."

"Who, me?"

He looks at me with irritation. "Yeah, you. Come on, dude." I walk outside and there she is, my dream. I am awestruck and I'm thankful that she speaks first.

"Hi."

"Hi, I'm Arshay."

"I'm Grace."

I say, "Yeah you are!" She laughs. I don't say anything else, I just look at her. There is nowhere in the world I want to be but right here, looking at her while she is looking back. I want to ask her to run away with me. There is an awkward moment and Preston says he is taking off. Grace says she has to go, too, and she looks up at me.

"Maybe you can walk me to the bus stop next week?" she asks.

"I like buses," I tell her, and she laughs.

"Okay, see you guys tomorrow."

"Have a good night, Miss Grace." I grab Preston by the shoulders and shake him. "Thank you, my brotha!"

We run back into the school and I am so excited to keep working on her poem. Preston heads to the gym for rowing, and I tell him I have to go to the office to call my mom and tell her I'm staying. When my mom answers, she tells me I can stay but she still hasn't heard from Shaundell. She called the school and he hasn't been there either. I hear the worry in her voice.

"Mom, did you pray?"

"Yes."

"Well, then, he is fine."

"Amen."

Preston and I walk into tryouts in the girls' gym room, and there are groups of kids scattered everywhere. Some are running around chasing one another, and others are shooting dice. The gym is small, with two hoops with our Wildcat logo sealed on the half-court line. We walk over to where we see kids sitting on this long gray machine with a sign on it that reads CONCEPT2. It looks like a motorcycle with a sliding seat and has a handle that you pull back and forth. I see Coach Jessica, the lady who was recruiting in the lunchroom, standing near them.

Preston hits me and whispers, "Boy, she fine as hell."

I see the terrible pretty boy, the one who threw the orange and jumped the kid, sitting on the machine going nuts, not knowing what the hell he is doing. Coach Jessica scrunches up her face like she doesn't know what she got herself into.

She walks over to the pretty boy. "What's your name?"

"Alvin Ross."

"Alvin, take it easy. That machine costs a lot of money," she says.

Alvin lets go of the handle and it flies toward the fan, hitting it with a loud clang. He hops off the machine in a huff. "Yeah, whatever, I can pay for that."

She looks like someone bust out her car windows as he walks away.

"Coach Jessica, what is this?" I ask.

"It's a rowing machine, or you can call it an erg machine," she replies. "I will tell you more about it in a few." She puts her hand around her mouth and yells, "Okay, everyone, listen up!"

No one listens and everyone keeps doing their thing. She looks at a black man standing in the corner and says, "Coach Victor, can you help?"

"Sure," he says calmly and whistles. Everyone stops.

"Bring it in!" she shouts.

We all gather around the Wildcat logo on the court and sit on the floor. There are about thirty of us, mostly boys and a few girls.

"Welcome to our last Manley Crew info session," Coach Jessica begins. "Today we aren't having tryouts, but that will happen soon. We want to start a team here that will offer swim lessons, tutoring, entrepreneurship, rowing competition, and access to college. We will expect you all to show up five days a week—four days of training, one day for entrepreneurship class or academic support. All we are looking for in tryouts is a work ethic and a five-day-a-week commitment to the team. Trust me, guys, it will be fun and you will have a chance to travel. After the coaches' introduction, we will give you handouts to take home with the date and time for tryouts."

"Sounds intense," Preston says, looking nervous.

"I want to introduce you guys to our strength-and-conditioning coach, Victor."

The bald black dude who whistled earlier waves. "Glad to be here, guys."

"I also want to introduce you to the sponsor behind this program, the man who came up with this idea, Ken Alpart."

I see a curly haired guy walk up. He's white and has a casual look. There's a hole in his T-shirt, and he's wearing run-down blue jeans and jacked-up tennis shoes. We give each other the side-eye. He starts talking, stumbling over his words a bit, but what he says is loud and clear.

"Crew is not for everyone."

A huge six-foot-tall freshman by the name of Malcolm yells out, "You mean black people?"

Everyone starts to laugh and Ken smirks a little bit. Preston tells Malcolm to let the man talk. I can't remember any all-black rowing team, so maybe Malcolm is right.

Ken continues. "It's a thinking man's sport. It doesn't matter if you have natural athletic abilities; what you need is discipline, commitment, focus, and the ability to work well with others. Michael Jordan wouldn't be the MVP for rowing, because in a boat of four or eight you will not notice one person, but a team. One unit. Everyone works as one. You will be noticed for your leadership outside the boat. You must be willing to work your butt off. This sport requires strong core balance, physical strength, flexibility, and cardiovascular endurance." Everyone is looking at him like he's speaking Greek, but Ken keeps going.

"I rowed in college at the University of Pennsylvania, and I think it's one of the most underrated and hardest sports around, if not *the* hardest. This is one of the oldest Olympic sports. There are no all-black public high school crew teams. *You* will be the first. This is a very white sport, as you saw on the television. We are not just trying to give you the opportunity to row. We want to give you the opportunity to think outside the box, be young entrepreneurs, go to Ivy League colleges, and travel the United States.

"Those who are serious will go to Philly on spring break and see what it is like to be a rower and a college student, and explore the city and hopefully check out a Race Regatta."

"Isn't that a cheese?" Preston whispers to me.

"No fool, that's ricotta," Malcolm responds.

Ken continues, "I went to Flower Career Academy, Marshall, and many public schools in the area with this idea and they all rejected it, saying this sport wasn't for their students, that it would not work. Mrs. Flanagan, the school principal, said yes. So if you do this with me, you will succeed. Hear that, you guys? You will succeed. Let's have a great year."

I look at Preston and say quietly, "Seems too good to be true."

"Maybe." He shrugs, still paying attention.

"I am pretty sure putting a group of black kids from our hood inside a boat to race white people is a setup for disaster."

"He said there's only one way to find out." Preston never takes his eyes off Ken. I can tell he's actually buying this speech.

I look around the gym and see students I know from the neighborhood and some I don't. These are the sons of drug addicts, prostitutes, gang members, and drug dealers. The people that we will race are possibly sons of lawyers, doctors, professors, and salesmen. I try to picture us in a boat next to them. I think about what the man told me at the barbershop. *Maybe I can succeed like these coaches are telling us.* Despite everything, I still believe in seizing the moment and that an opportunity is a gift. My mother taught me that.

I lean over to Preston one more time. "Where do we sign up?"

3

In Sync

My armpits are sweaty, which only happens when I'm nervous. It's the first real day of rowing tryouts and I keep saying to myself, "*Be strong and confident, and do it afraid,*" as I walk toward the gym.

There are more than a dozen people present, including Ken, Coach Jessica, and Coach Victor. Tryouts are inside the small girls' basketball gymnasium. The erg machines are lined up across the gym floor like an army of pawns and now I am stoked to demonstrate my power. I look around and see all the boys wearing basketball shorts and T-shirts with cut-off sleeves. There are no girls today. Coach Jessica walks over and holds a clipboard up to me. "Hey, sign in here," she says brightly. "What's your name?"

"Arshay Cooper."

"That's unique; what does it mean?"

"I don't know, but there is a song that goes 'funga alafia ashay ashay.' That's the closest thing I know."

She chuckles to herself. "Well, you should find out."

Coach Victor is speaking with Ken, who is wearing the same clothes he had on the last time I saw him. The guys here are very cliquish. A group of upperclassmen are all huddled together. I recognize Arthur, Elliot, and Marcus. They are into video games and comic-book shit. In the corner of the gym is this guy, Danny, and a couple others I really don't know. They were shooting dice during the info session, and their dark lips have "pothead" written all over them. Preston is by the door spitting game to some girl in the hallway. I look over at Alvin and think, *Why isn't this dude outside beating on someone or stealing something?* He seriously makes me feel uneasy.

Coach Victor whistles and shouts, "Practice is starting!"

We huddle around the center court, ready to let the beast out. I am wearing black jogging pants and a big shirt I got from the thrift store in the Little Village neighborhood for two bucks. It's a little too big for me and looks like its dangling on a hanger when I have it on.

"I want to welcome you guys today. I'm excited for today's practice," Coach Victor says with relish. "Listen, guys, as a black man looking at other young black men, introducing you to the sport of rowing is a wish granted. You may say to yourself, I can't swim! I don't do water! It's okay. We will teach you, because every time you conquer a fear, life gets a lot less scary."

Victor turns and meets my eyes with his. "Or you may have looked at the video in the lunchroom and thought to yourself, I don't belong. But you do, because the history of sports has proven that. Take advantage of this because opportunities are for people who need them, and those who show up to get them."

Damn, I want to shout hallelujah. Everyone nods to Victor's speech. Malcolm, the big freshman, looks suspicious.

"Today, we are going to stretch, warm up, get on the erg, and circle up to talk team goals. Okay, guys?"

All the guys start whooping excitedly.

"Before we start, I want to be clear that practice starts directly after school at 3:00 Monday through Friday, and ends at 4:30. You are expected to wear a T-shirt and shorts or sweatpants until you earn that

Manley uniform. You will obtain that by showing up, working hard, and being a team player." Coach Victor means serious business.

"Okay, everyone, stand and hands up straight. Now reach down and touch your toes."

"Stretching is for homos," Malcolm yells out.

"What you say?" Coach Victor yells.

"Stretching is for hoes!" Malcolm yells back. Everyone laughs.

Malcolm says whatever the hell he wants. He is one of those guys who smacks food out of your hands and you do nothing about it because he's so big. He stands six foot four feet tall and has to be about 230 pounds, which will probably make him a killer on our team. He comes from a family of Muslims and is one of ten kids. I'm excited and terrified to have him as a teammate, and I wonder if Coach Victor will be able to manage him.

Coach Victor looks pissed off and stares directly at Malcolm. "I'll tell you about the importance of stretching and who it's for. We stretch to prevent injuries and to prepare our bodies for a workout. Rowing requires you using your full body, and stretching will enhance your performance. Got it?" His tone cuts through the rowdy group and silences Malcolm for now. Everyone nods and starts to stretch.

When we finish up, Coach barks another order. "Okay, guys, run twenty laps around the gym while the coaches step outside to talk."

The guys yell out, "Twenty laps? Forget that!"

Coach Jessica chimes in, "Come on, guys, it's a small gym, you will be finished in no time. You got this."

Everyone likes Coach Jessica. She is down-to-earth and I heard people say she is a master team rower. She doesn't seem to play games and you can tell she is tough as nails. When she stretches with us, the guys can't keep their eyes off of her, especially Preston. I think he's in love. Everyone's eyes are on her as the coaches walk out of the gym.

Preston finally looks away as the doors clatter shut and grabs a basketball. "Let's run a full-court game." Preston passes the ball to me hard, and the guys jump into action. The squeak of our sneakers echoes around the gym and we are caught up in the game until the door swings open again. "Hey! Get back to running!"

Preston stops mid-layup. "But this is cardio," he pleads.

Ken's frown gives way to laughter. "Well, the kid may have a point," he says to Jessica.

"Nope. Get back to running," Coach Jessica says.

Twenty laps later, we are ready to die. None of us is in shape. We drag ourselves over to the erg machine, where Jessica is going to give us a demonstration. She sits down on it as Preston and a couple of the other guys drool and stare at a rip in her pants.

"Sitting on an erg is like sitting on the boat," she instructs. "And being in a boat is like being in a shell, a very narrow shell." She bends her knees and reaches for the handle as the seat slides forward. She stretches as far as she can, until her head is past her knees. A murmur runs through the group as we admire how flexible she is. All the guys think it's pretty sexy and I'm sure she can see us smiling.

"Now, guys, I am at the catch. When you row in a boat you have the choice to start off this way. When I say row, I am going to push back with my legs, then swing back with my body, and pull with my arms. When I complete that movement, I'm at the finish. Why is it called the finish?"

"Because you finished a stroke," I say, unsure.

"Correct, Arshay," she chirps. "Now, on the way back to the catch, you will do the opposite. Arms out, body forward, and break legs away."

Jessica shouts, "Row!" and drives back with power. Her body moves smoothly as she demonstrates how to use the machine. "If you hear the fan going, you are working.

"Okay, guys, grab a machine and let's row. Ken, Victor, and I will walk around and help you."

I get on a machine and start to pull. It feels good. I can feel my legs, core, arms, chest, and shoulders burn all at the same time. Ken walks over to me and gives me some pointers. I ask him if I will get this in a day, and he assures me that it will take some time.

He assures me I'll get it with practice and turns to join the other coaches who've gathered around Malcolm. His strokes rock the machine like he's out on the water, and all the coaches have to hold it down. I can tell the coaches are impressed by how strong he is.

After a few minutes the pain starts to settle in, but I can feel my muscles growing. Ten more minutes and I'm beat and sweating through my T-shirt. Coach Jessica calls for a five-minute water break, and everyone jumps up and makes a beeline to the vending machines.

"No, no, no!" the coaches yell as we return with our snacks.

They come running toward us and Ken snatches the Flamin' Hot Cheetos out of my hand and the other coaches collect the grape and orange sodas from everyone else.

"You're going to mess up your workout!" Ken yells.

"What? How?" I ask him, confused.

Everyone is pissed, and I see Alvin ball his fist up like he is going to knock someone out.

Ken launches into a speech about nutrition. He explains the food chart, and talks about the body and what it needs and doesn't need. I'm surprised when he tells us that fried food isn't healthy. All I know is that it tastes *good*. This is the first time I've heard words like *protein, carbs, calories,* and their definitions.

"I want you guys to eat good carbs in the morning, like oatmeal. You can also have eggs and beans with wheat bread for breakfast. Chicken, brown rice, and vegetables are good for lunch and dinner."

I'm not sure if he knows that we can't afford this stuff and that the school lunch is greasy and nowhere close to the food he's talking about, but he will soon. A look of uncertainty spreads around the guys in the gym.

"The body is like a Jaguar," he continues. "For it to go fast, you must put the right fuel in it. Food is our fuel. We must put the proper grub in our bodies for success and strength." I understand what he is saying, but the truth is we will eat whatever the school serves and what our family can afford. I know the guys all want to look good, have a six-pack, and live a long life, but it's more complicated than that. Still, we promise Ken that we'll try to eat better.

Break is over and we get back on the erg machines. The Flamin' Hot Cheetos are sitting heavy in my stomach. I place my feet into the foot stretcher and tighten it up. I grab the handle, and Coach Victor sets the monitor to open distance, telling me to go until I can't anymore.

"Let's work on your technique and find your pace," he says. I grab the handle and sit at the finish while Coach Victor stands over me.

"Sit tall and chin up," Victor says. "Now, row."

I rush to the catch and swing back fast.

"Okay, settle in. Do you see this number right here on the right-hand corner of your meter box?" He points. "That's how many strokes you are going per minute. You are at thirty-four; that is too fast." I stop and the handle snaps forward. "No, don't stop," he yells. I pick the handle back up and pull, steady this time. "You are at 32; now slow down to a 24." I slow down. "Come up to the catch patiently and drive back with pressure and speed."

My thoughts are all over the place trying to coordinate every move my body makes. I'm overthinking, and it is all happening too fast. "Okay, Arshay. Slow, now drive! Slow, now drive! There it is, you at a 24. Now settle in. Breath on the recovery and push on the drive. Don't pull, push." My mind and body find a rhythm with his coaching, and I start to feel good at this pace, my breath no longer heaving. Coach Victor points to the middle of the rowing screen as I drive again and again.

"See this big number that looks like the time?" I nod my head yes, unable to get the words out. "That's your 500-meter split. The harder you drive, the lower that time drop. Right now, you're at 2:15. Let's take it down to 2:00. On your drive, push harder and maintain your technique."

Everything is coming into place, but my muscles strain with the effort. I watch my split drop to a 1:50. "Okay, Arshay, keep it there. Maintain it. Good job." He walks away. My body is telling me to stop, but I can't. I've been through harder shit than this.

In the background I can hear Coach Victor doing the same drill with everyone else.

"Way enough!" he finally calls out, which is the signal we can finally stop. Sweat runs down my face—everyone is gasping for air and coughing. I slip my feet out of the stretchers and my chest hits my knees as I fold.

Preston walks over toward me, holding his back. "This good shit, Coop."

"Joe, I'm tired," I say, gasping.

"Two months of this and you gonna shred."

I laugh. "That's the plan."

"Okay, everyone on the erg for the last part of the practice," says Coach Jessica after only a few minutes' rest.

"Damn, again? These damn people gonna kill us," Preston says, walking back to his erg.

Coach Jessica stands over Preston. "Everyone is going to follow Preston this time."

"She loves my stroke, oh hell naw," Preston sings.

Laughter fills the room.

"*Preston!*" Coach Victor yells.

"Just having fun, Coach," Preston says, tossing his hands up.

"Alright, everyone to the catch," Coach Jessica demands.

"You guys are going to follow Preston and learn to move together. That is what rowing is all about. When he is at the catch, you are at the catch, and when he is at the finish, you are, too.

"Okay?" Half of the group nods. "Ready, set, row." We all are pushing, but timing is not quite on our side.

"Arshay, you are off," Malcolm shouts.

"Dude, don't worry about me," I call back.

"Preston, slow the hell down," Alvin yells.

"If we can pack fifty black students in a room to do the electric slide together, we should be able to do this," Malcolm says in a huff.

I gag and laugh, also in a huff. We keep rowing as the coaches walk around the room to help.

"At a twenty-four," Coach Jessica tells Preston. "Listen to the sound of the fan; it tells you when you're recovering and when you're on the drive. Just listen."

We are starting to get it, and everyone's focused and tuned in.

"Recover, catch!" she calls repeatedly.

We fall in sync, and it's only the first day. Satisfaction ripples through the air. I'm getting thirsty for the feeling of being on the water, each stroke driving a magical rhythm. After a while, Coach Jessica says, "On my call, way enough in two strokes. One, two. Way enough. Good job. Okay, guys, bring it in."

Everyone hops off the machines—fatigued but buzzing with excitement.

Ken passes out a sheet of paper and calls for our attention. "Give yourself a hand." Everyone starts clapping. "The feeling of accomplishment that you have right now is the feeling you should have every day of your life. Today, you did it." Ken continues, "This year's goals are to get you in shape this fall, pass the swim test this winter, get on the water in the spring with a possible spring-break trip, and race the spring and summer season against some private school kids." We all start screaming and pounding the floor. "But, most importantly, get your grades up, learn about starting a business, go to college, and be contributors to your community. We want you to be student athletes. Have a good day. See you tomorrow, and bring a friend." He turns to huddle with the other coaches.

I hear a rise of voices behind me.

"Y'all read this?" Malcolm says. I look down at the sheet Ken passed out.

1. What size shoes do you wear?
2. Do you like Air Jordan shoes?
3. Have you ever flown on an airplane?
4. What size shirt do you wear?
5. What is your favorite video game?
6. Have you been to a Chicago Bulls game?

A roar of excitement fills the gymnasium as everyone starts giving high fives.

"I'm finally getting some Jordans."

"I want first-class seats."

"I'm taking my girl to the Bulls game."

I bolt out of the gym to my locker to find a dry shirt. I grab one that smells like cooking lard and throw it on.

I glide toward the staircase, feeling like I am a part of something. Practice was different than other classes at Manley, where teachers focus on your shortcomings. Today, someone paid attention to my strengths. I'm all charged up, and then I see Grace with her friends walking up the stairs. Seeing her come toward me is like being on the erg all over again; my pulse is going crazy and I can't catch my breath.

"Hey, Arshay," she says softly. She stops, and all her friends do, too.

"I'm good," I say, unprompted. *Oh my God, so stupid,* I think to myself. Grace's friends are looking at me like I am wearing a clown outfit.

"Last time I saw you, we talked about walking to the bus stop." I gulp, going right for it. "If that's cool?" I want to get out of here and away from her friends before I embarrass myself.

"Tomorrow?" she asks.

"I'm down!"

"Okay, see you tomorrow then." She walks away with her friends.

I slide down the school banister like Bart Simpson. Now I know what Ice Cube meant when he said, *"Today was a good day."*

4

Grace

I get home and find my mom sitting at the kitchen table. She points to the chair across from her and tells me to have a seat. *Oh God, what now?* She tells me that Shaundell called to say he is fine.

I yell, "I told you!" triumphantly. I move to go to my room, but she tells me to sit back down.

"Arshay, he's moving out to your grandmother's."

"Mom, you yourself said if we can't handle the rules then we have to leave."

"Yeah, but is it that hard?" she asks me.

"No, but no one wants to get up and sing songs every morning."

"But if it was the WGCI radio station you guys would be singing them in the morning as you get ready."

I laugh and agree.

My mom sits quietly for a minute and then gets up out of her chair.

"Listen, I know I've messed up in the past, big-time. But I am a different person now. We have dinner together. I work, I provide. Well, God provides. I am going to go down as a testimony. From the moment my eyes was open from my addiction, I done everything a mom was supposed to do according to God's word."

"You are, Mom. Look at Vince. He was a gang leader, but now he is working on getting out, going to church with us. Uncle Terry is at the Victory Outreach home in California about to graduate. Aunt Jennifer stopped doing drugs the moment she witnessed your change and now she is going to church. Aunt Tina is now getting involved in church. Your whole family, Mom."

She sits quietly, looking at me, weighing my words.

"It's all because of you; your prayers and spirituality. Religion couldn't do that! All I know is that I didn't believe in anything, but now I believe in something and it lives in you. Mom, you always tell people, 'Train up a child in the way he should go, and they will never depart from it.'

"It doesn't mean we aren't going to make mistakes or want to move out, it means what we learn will always be inside of us. And when it's time to change, we won't need a book or an altar—we will already know what to do. You didn't teach us the way we should go, but you truly trained us; we living it!"

She looks at me with soft eyes and says what she always says: "How did you turn out so good?"

I say what I always say back to her. "I was going to ask you the same."

"Arshay, tell me how the rowing stuff is going. I remember glancing at the flyer."

"It's no big deal, Mom."

"No, tell me, Arshay."

"We are not on the water yet or anything, but the machines are cool and get you fit."

"Oh, look at my baby, going to be strong and all," she says proudly.

"Well, I will let you know if I stick with it." I shrug.

"Son, you better. I have a feeling about this one. Just don't get your butt out there and drown."

I laugh. "I won't drown, Mom." I get up from the table and give her a smile before walking down the hall to my room. It's time to work on my poem for Grace, while I'm still high off of practice.

Today was a good day.

The next morning, I am actually excited to go to school. There are only three things that can make me excited to go to school: a class trip, a home basketball game against a rival, or a girl. I'm not looking forward to my classes, just Grace.

Manley has been vibrant these last couple of weeks. Everyone is walking around with their Walkmans, going crazy over Wu-Tang, Bone Thugs-n-Harmony, Aaliyah, Do or Die, and Twista. Hip-hop and R & B are what we breathe, think, and dream. It even controls our decision making at times. If I am listening to Ginuwine, I want to kiss somebody. If it's Do or Die, I'm looking to smoke. Montell Jordan has me ready to sneak out my window to party, and if it's Kirk Franklin, we are praying. Almost every dude comes to school carrying a basketball or football and wearing their red and black school colors. Teachers would love for it to be a book, but they're thankful it's not a gun.

By last period I can't concentrate on what I am going to say to Grace while I walk her to the bus stop. Everything I think of seems lame. After thinking too much, I decide I will freestyle. The bell rings and I walk downstairs to wait for her. A couple minutes later, I can hear her saying good-bye to the security guards, teachers, students, and anyone she walks by. *Heaven must be like this.* She sees me and we lock eyes and smile.

"Hey, how was class?" she asks.

"Better than yesterday."

She laughs. She always laughs.

She asks, "Shall we?" I take the bookbag from her arms.

I can tell she's impressed, as if no boy has done that before. We start walking down West Polk Street toward South Kedzie Avenue, and I ask her about her classes and the cheerleading team. It is all about her and I am happy to let her talk. It's like listening to my favorite song. I walk slowly because we are only going two blocks.

When we get to the next street, a car with five guys inside pulls up. In the driver's seat is the guy with the box haircut who pulled out a gun the day the S.O.A. gang jumped that kid. He yells out, "Grace, come here, let me holla at you."

"No, I'm good."

"Come on, you got a boyfriend or what?"

"I'm good."

I can't decide whether or not I should say something. I'm walking a very thin line. On one hand, I want to be a man and be hard and show Grace I'm not a punk. On the other, I need to be strategic. If Grace is smart, she'll know these guys are trouble and that they want to bait me into a fight.

To my relief, she says, "Don't mind them. That is so disrespectful."

They speed away and I feel an urgent need to get out of the hood. I'm willing to do whatever it takes to leave, but the hood is all I know.

We get to the bus stop and wait. I'm praying silently that the bus won't come.

"So, you are on that rowing team, right?"

"Yeah, I am."

"Tell me about it."

"It's a white sport, you know."

"So what's a white sport and what's a black sport?" she asks.

"I think black sports are the ones that are cheap to play. Like, all you need is a ball or a glove. White sports cost a lot and require boats, ergs, or horses."

She laughs and says, "What else?"

"We have three coaches: Victor, he's black and everyone loves him. Then there's Jessica, who is tough and Preston can't keep his eyes off her.

Then Ken, who is the sponsor. So he is probably super-rich, and he said we are the first all-black public high school team. Wait, am I talking too much?" I say nervously.

"No, no, you're fine."

"Am I?"

"Ha ha, good one, Arshay."

"More to come, Grace."

"Well, my bus is a block away. I hope that you stick with rowing."

"I am. I am also writing this poem for you."

"Let's see it."

"Not yet."

"Okay, I can't wait to read it." She hugs me and steps onto the bus.

"Tomorrow?" I ask her, and she looks back and smiles.

"Tomorrow."

I run back to school for rowing practice, practically floating. When I get to the gym, I tell Preston what happened.

"Did you get a number?"

"No. Why? I am going to see her in school tomorrow."

"Man, get that number and try to hit that!" I laugh and tell him to chill out because I know what I'm doing. Then I get an idea.

"We should take Grace and her friend Lisa on a double date."

Alvin walks up. "Lisa who?"

I turn around and look at him, in shock that he heard us. He is the troublemaker I saw jumping the kid outside the school, and I don't want anything to do with him.

"Nobody."

"I heard you, homie. Lisa who?"

Preston tells him, "Light-skin Lisa."

Alvin asks if Preston is messing around with her, because he is, too. I'm nervous because I'm sure there's about to be trouble. Preston just laughs and says, "Yeah," and then they're shaking hands and sharing details.

I decide it isn't my business and start warming up on the erg.

"Okay, everyone, let's get off the ergs and gather at center court," Ken yells from the middle of the gym. Today, twenty people showed up to practice. Five girls and fifteen boys. All the girls are joking around with one another, so they must be friends already. Coach Jones, the athletic director, is here checking out the practice. She is the most relaxed and no-nonsense coach of the staff in the building. College ball was her thing, and she stands about six-two. Coach Jones is also the girl's basketball and volleyball coach and is a school favorite. Ken had to go through her to start this team for sure.

"Today, we will start with some teambuilding to get to know each other a little bit," Ken says. I only know a few guys, so teambuilding games work for me.

"My name is Ken Alpart, and I am thirty-two years old. I am an options and futures trader. I started my own company, Alpart Trading, in downtown Chicago. I founded Urban Options, a foundation dedicated to working with kids on Chicago's West Side. I am all about giving my time, talent, and treasure to local Little League baseball teams, hockey teams, and now the crew team. My good friend Mike O'Gorman, a national team coach, actually came up with the idea to start a rowing team on the West Side. So we are. I also teach a youth entrepreneurship class once a week on the West Side. I have a wife, Jennifer Bonjean, who is a law school student, and we have a beautiful little girl named Winnifred." Preston walks up and gives Ken a fist bump. "'And that's the way we became the Brady Bunch,'" Ken says, laughing as he receives the fist bump.

"Alright, everyone," Ken says, raising his right hand. "You will find someone on this team you don't know and introduce yourself as I did. One person goes, then the other. You have one minute each. Now go."

I notice that there are guys here from different gangs, so they try to avoid one another. I bypass Alvin. I find myself with Danny, who has never spoken to me. He is straight hood. He is just a little taller than me, with a nose that looks like it's been fractured a few times. He is always shooting dice in the hallways and before practice. He is wearing a black hoodie and some black shorts. Danny's Afro could use a weed wacker; it hasn't been combed in months.

"Hey, Danny," I start.

"How you know my name?" he says aggressively.

"Danny, I know your name because you are on the crew team."

"Why you talk like that?"

"Like what?"

"Like a white boy or some shit."

"Dude that's ignorant, you mean proper English?" I feel myself becoming irritated.

"Man, just do your piece because you don't want none," Danny says violently.

"My name is Arshay—" and I stop because this fool just turned and walked away as I was speaking and joined a group of three where his friends are. *That didn't go well*, I say to myself and shuffle over to Preston.

"Okay, time!" Ken shouts. "Now find someone else and spend one minute telling them why you joined the team."

I search for someone cool, and this guy grabs me.

"Hey bruh, my name is Terry." Now, this guy is jolly and chunky. All he needs are gifts, and I will be calling him Santa.

"I'm Arshay, and I joined the team because I wanted to try something new, find new friends, and travel." It was also because of Preston hooking it up with Grace, but there is no need to mention that.

"That's it?" Terry says.

"That's it," I reply.

"Well, look at me," Terry says. "I am fat, so my number-one business is to get in shape." I laugh because he says it so boldly. "I don't have a ton of friends; I want to stay out of trouble, and Ken gave us that paper about the Jordans and stuff. So yeah, I'm gonna need those."

"Right on." I shake Terry's hand and say welcome to the team. We go on and on for what feels like an hour until we meet almost everyone on the squad. The questions become more serious and my eyes start to open to the different lives of my schoolmates. I learned about the murder of Elliot's mom, that Ronald is going to the army after high school, Malcolm has ten siblings, Terry wants to avoid the gangs, Erica's dad is in jail for a crime he didn't commit, and it goes on. The activity was engaging, exciting, challenging, and creative. The gift that we gave each other was to listen.

For the last half hour of practice, we fly through our usual routine of stretching, laps, and rowing pick drills. After training, Coach Jessica tells us to stick around for some good news. We sit at the half-court line, waiting.

"There will be a team trip next Saturday to the University of Wisconsin," Coach Jessica says. Everyone gets mad charged.

"Is it overnight and are we flying?" I ask.

"No, we will take a van, and it's only for the day. We will tour the campus, and they have what we call a 'rowing tank.' It is an indoor facility that will help you understand what it is like to row on the water. Once you use this, you will have an idea of what it's like to row."

More questions start flying everywhere.

"Will I drown?"

"Can I bring my girl?"

"Do I need money?"

"No, to all those things. Please come up to get your permission slip, and you can be dismissed."

When I watch the news, I see that kids are dying, going to jail, and not receiving a good education. Those kids are us in this room. We still have students come to practice once and then never come back, and the coaches seem to be figuring things out as they go, but the Manley Crew Team feels as though it's coming together. We have a steady fifteen with a couple of girls: Preston, Alvin, Terry, Malcolm, Ronald, Danny, Arthur,

Marcus, Leslie, Tanika, Elliot, Dashun, Pheodus, Antwon, and me. It takes a village to raise a child, and our village is gang members, drug dealers, drug addicts, and prostitutes. It's easy to become a product of this, but I feel like the coaches are using rowing to get us into college and to change our village.

5

Like Water

We pull up to the University of Wisconsin on a colorful fall Saturday, and are met by a gigantic sign that reads BE A BADGER. We get out of the van and Coach Victor directs us to the admissions office. The tree leaves match the caramel-and-cinnamon-brick colors of the school. In the garden, I see a big *W* engraved in the walkway. Everyone is wearing red Wisconsin sweaters and appears to be happy as hell. Students are playing Frisbee, lying on the lawn reading, and seating in groups talking. It doesn't seem like a lot of excitement is kicking off during the school hour, but it sure feels peaceful. I've only ever seen this on TV, and never in a million years thought I would be on a college campus.

We tour the campus with a super-cute and anxious freckle-face college sophomore, and all the questions come from the three seniors—Ronald, Arthur, and Marcus. Arthur, who looks like a mini bodybuilder, doesn't say much in practice but has an insane work ethic and can do cardio for days. When I am hanging on for dear life after a workout, he looks unfazed. Arthur asks the question everyone has been itching to find out. "What is it like to be a black man on this campus?"

Everyone is dead silent.

"Um, I don't personally know, but there is a black student union that does cool stuff on campus, and we believe in diversity and inclusion here and hope you consider joining our school." She looks like she is ready for a nap after that.

"See, they should have had a black student leading this," Malcolm whispers to the group in the back.

"We have Coach Victor here," Marcus says.

The tour ends and the girl thanks us for coming.

"Boy, that black man can't do everything," Malcolm says, as we head to the athletic center to see the tanks.

Elliot and I begin talking as we walk across campus. "Can you imagine being away like this and not living on the West Side?" he asks passionately.

"I imagine stuff like this daily, joe. But I don't play basketball or football, you know."

"I feel you, but I am gonna do it getting in these books."

"Elliot, I'm not a dream killer, but everyone says that and ends up getting a job in the hood."

"Well, not me, Arshay. Look at this place; ain't nobody getting shot over here."

"True, it would be gravy to live in a place where you don't have to watch every shadow. I need a life road map or something on how to get here. Nobody in my family has ever gone to college. Teachers try to help, but they're busy breaking up fights and teaching us how to survive," I tell Elliot, really feeling the conversation.

"Yeah, let's try to survive Manley first," Elliot adds.

"Gotch."

The coaches begin talking to us about what college is like and how we would have the best years of our life if we decide to go. "Hey, Coach Victor, who paid for us to come here?" Malcolm asks.

"Ken. So thank him when you see him."

Malcolm says, "This school is cool, but way too many white people."

Preston tells him he's a black racist.

"No such thing; I'm a black realist."

I just laugh at them both. They stay on each other's case.

We walk into the athletic facility pumped. As we check out the place, we see a big wrestling mat, and everyone instantly transforms into WWF mode. We decide to go at each other Royal Rumble style. Malcolm is slamming everyone, so I tell him I will wrestle him.

"You don't want none," Malcolm says.

"We both are the two strongest on the erg, but let's settle it here," I reply.

Everyone is rooting for me and screaming my name. Malcolm is looking like he's done this before as he stands in fighting position.

No one makes a move; we stare.

I charge him and grab his leg, and he slams me right on my back, and everyone starts laughing. Without a doubt, he is the strongest and scariest guy on the team, I think to myself while lying there. I get up and tell him he's strong, but not so tough.

"We'll prove it on the next erg race."

"Okay, whatever." He shrugs.

There are nine of us on this trip. Preston, Malcolm, Arthur, Elliot, Marcus, Ronald, Terry, Danny, and myself. We are the serious ones. I am not sure why Alvin didn't make it, but I'm distracted as we head down to the rowing tank. We see the tank and all run toward it like we are at a water theme park. We have been spending so much time on the erg that we thirst to see some version of the water, and this reminds us that we are a step closer. I am most excited to have an oar in my hand. I have never seen anything like this, and it will be the first time we can go full throttle together as one. The tank looks like a giant pool that mimics an erg seat, slide, and footplate next to it. The red and white blades are already on top of the tank. We are so excited that we hop in right away.

Coach Jessica says, "Okay, guys, grab your oar. An oar is used to move the boat. Oars are long poles with one flat end that is called the *blade* or *spoon.* The spoon of the oar is normally painted with the colors of the club to which it belongs. It identifies boats at a distance."

"So ours would be red and black," I tell her.

"Yep, that's a great combo," she replies. "There are two types of rowing. There is *sculling,* which requires two oars per person, and there is *sweep,* which has one oar per rower. We will be rowing in a sweep. Now, each rower is referred to as a *port* or a *starboard,* depending on which side of the boat the rower's oar extends to.

"If your oar is to your left, you are a starboard, and if the oar is to your right, you are a port. You can row in pairs, fours, or eights. The goal is to have an eight-person team and a four-person team. Rowers have other titles and roles. In an eight-plus boat, the stern pair is responsible for setting the stroke rate for the rhythm of the boat to follow. They lead. The middle four are usually the less technical, but more powerful in the crew. The bow pair is the more technical and set up the balance of the boat. Last, you have the coxswain."

Preston interrupts her mid-speech. "The cock's what?" Everyone starts laughing and Coach Jessica tells him his mind is always in the gutter.

"The coxswain is the person who usually sits in the stern of the boat, facing the bow. They coordinate the power and rhythm of the rowers. This must be a light-weighted person."

She tells us she wants the stern pair to come up the catch. "You guys learn this in the gym on the erg machine. It's the same motion, but you just have an oar."

She gives us the signal and we start rowing. She adds on the next two rowers, and the two after that, until we are all working in sync. It's a beautiful experience. We start to feel what it'd be like to row on the water one day. I look around at everyone's faces and start to believe this might actually work.

"Way enough!" she shouts. You can tell that everyone feels good to be a part of something and we're all happy to be out of the neighborhood.

I can't believe one hour has passed already, and it's time to head home. Walking back to the car, I am all smiles.

"Coach Victor, had you traveled in high school?"

"Not like you guys are going to."

"I have always wanted to travel without being in the army or navy."

"You will have plenty of opportunities, being on the first all-black public high school row team."

"We're in the late '90s, I can't believe that first black anything still exists."

"Tell me about it." He laughs.

On our way home, Preston asks if I want to hang with him on the West Side in the old neighborhood for a little bit.

"No, that's not me anymore. There is nothing over there for me."

"Your old friends, they always ask about you. Don't forget where you come from."

"I don't forget," I tell him, "that's why I don't go back."

"I want it to be like old times, when all of us just kicked it on the porch doing nothing."

"I get it, but I don't wanna be in the wrong place at the wrong time. And there won't be a wrong time if I can avoid the wrong place. I won't be hanging out on the corner or some porch no more, and that's just the way it is. Plus, I don't want to deal with Big T."

He shakes his head slowly and tells me it's all good. I realize that people get upset when you put you first.

When I get dropped off at home I see a man walking around inside with his shirt off. It's my stepfather, Ike. I haven't seen him since he got locked up. My hands hit my knees as I hunch over like MJ does in between free throws. But I am gasping for air. Memories rush through me like a runaway train. I sit down on the stoop and start thinking back to when I was a kid; I spent a lot of time with Ike while Shaundell spent time with my grandfather. Ike would take me to the grocery store with him and try to teach me how to hustle. "When a person comes out with a cart, don't ask to help carry the bags, just grab it and say, 'Where is your car?' If they give you less than a dollar you say, 'What's this?'"

He was always telling me, "You have to hustle to make it in this world." He never once taught me anything about love, reading, loyalty, math, or faith.

Ike once asked Shaundell and me if we wanted to play outside. He had us stand on the corner and dribble the basketball.

"And if you see a police car, scream, 'Hey, mama!'"

It sounded easy enough, so we obliged, not knowing we were part of his street team while he sold drugs on the block.

There were times I was in the car with him and he would stop in the middle of the street. He'd walk over to other cars and tell them we'd run out of gas and ask them to help us. "My son is just sitting in the car, scared," he'd tell them, while I just sat in the car, confused.

I never said anything. I kept everything inside.

I wipe the sweat off my face and straighten up, catching my breath. I need to pull it together. I walk into the apartment and see Ike sitting tall at the table like he pays bills here. His muscular frame is imposing in the space. I think about the long scar that runs down his stomach. I know he just got out of jail.

I walk over and shake his hand.

"Hey, 'sup, man?"

"Just got out and happy to be home," he says in his low, raspy voice.

"Really?" I ask him. "I thought jail was home."

"Come on, man, I am trying to change," he tells me.

I tell him that trying isn't good enough.

"Well, I'm going to church with you guys Sunday."

I tell him that's good, and that it's good to see him, and walk into the bedroom I share with Isaac. My mom and Pamela share the front room, so I can't figure out where Ike is going to sleep.

He yells after me that he wants to catch up and hear about my grades.

"For sure," I yell back, slamming the door.

I sit on my mattress and think of the night Ike got that large scar on his stomach. I was ten, sitting on the couch watching TV. My mother was in the front room, screaming at Ike through the door. He was in the hallway outside the apartment, pleading, "Why would you leave me? I love you!"

"Leave me alone," she screamed back, "it's over. I will call the police if you don't leave."

"If you don't open this door, I will kill myself. I am not playing around."

"That's your business, but I want nothing to do with you, Ike."

Ike got louder. "I'm going to kill myself. I can't live without you, Linda."

My mom didn't say anything. Ike told me through the door that if I didn't open it, he really would kill himself. I sat there quietly waiting until my mom turned her head, then ran quickly to the door to try to open it. I got as far as the knob, and my mom grabbed my arm and threw me across the room as she yelled at me. I remember hitting my head on the wall and hearing Ike say, "Linda . . . your son!" Everything got smaller, darkness closed in, and then I blacked out.

When I opened my eyes I heard my mom screaming and saw Ike standing there with his stomach cut open. I could see his insides hanging out.

My mom was hysterical. "Oh my God, he did it! He did it!" I backed up to the wall with my head on my knees and closed my eyes. I blocked out the noise, the smell, everything, and imagined falling. There was nothing else to think about. That day put a hole in my heart that I didn't know how to fix.

Ike had his issues, but there were good memories, too. He would let me sit on his lap while he was driving, showing me what to do. I remember him bringing food home. He would stop my mom from hitting us with extension or telephone cords when she would beat us until our skin ripped open.

The memories slowly slip away and I come back out of my room and join everyone at the kitchen table. Mom cooked some pork chops and Rice-A-Roni. Everyone is at the dinner table except Shaundell. I wish he were here. Being the only protector of my mom is terrifying right now.

"Ike, Arshay is on the first all-black public high school rowing team," Isaac says. My mom beams.

"Rowing?" Ike asks, looking stunned.

"Yes, rowing," I reply.

"That canoeing shit? What white folks got you doing that?"

"That's what I said," Isaac adds.

"Linda, what school he goes to? Imma talk to that damn principal."

"It's okay, Ike," my mom says. Sitting here is more torching than an episode of *M*A*S*H*, I think to myself.

"I just don't want this boy to drown," Ike says passionately.

"I am not going to drown."

"Can you swim?" Ike says, staring at me.

"I am going to learn."

"Oh shit, Linda, the boy can't swim."

"No cursing at the table, Daddy," my little sister says.

"Okay, baby," Ike assures her.

"Arshay, play one of those ball sports that will make you some money to hold down this family."

"I am holding down this family!" I shout.

My mom slams her hands on the table. "*I'm* holding down this family. Now let's eat." You can hear a feather drop; it's so quiet.

Ike starts sharing prison stories. "You know, Arshay and Isaac, jail is not the place to be. One day for breakfast, they feed us a donut and mash potatoes," he says while holding a pork chop in one hand and the bottle of hot sauce in the other, and pouring it on his meat after every bite.

"Is that why we shouldn't go?" Isaac says, smirking. I just can't believe Ike is at the dinner table with his shirt off. I would never get away with that.

"There are many reasons you shouldn't go," Ike continues, ignoring Isaac's attitude. "I saw young boys in there getting raped and they couldn't protect themselves because they have never thrown a punch a day in their lives. They made one mistake and they are never going home. People are being tossed in the hole, in complete darkness, and come out not knowing what month it is. I was roommates with someone who has *Life* for killing two people in bright daylight and told me I better sleep with one eye open. Isaac, every day someone is going behind bars for a crime they didn't commit. They have never even broken a plate. That's why you shouldn't go."

"So why do you keep going in?" I ask. Mom chokes.

"You okay, baby?" Ike says quietly. "I grew up in a home with no food. Similar to you, but worse. So, I went to a church with my buddy, Guy, and I stole a couple of purses so I could eat.

"I wasn't even old enough to smoke or drink. Just wanted to eat. Honestly. Got locked up and had a public defender who couldn't tell you what color my eyes were. When I got out, I couldn't find a job because of my record. So, I went to the only place that will hire me, the drug dealer down the block. He bought me my first gold chain and my first car."

I stare down at my plate.

Mom finally breaks the silence. "Okay, let's enjoy our food."

After we finish dinner, I head outside to chat with Ike while he smokes a cigarette. He tells me, "I'm still tripping off your mother. She is a changed woman that *loves going to church*! Who would have ever thought?"

"I know," I reply.

"You know I'm a Christian, right? I went to chapel every day," he says proudly.

"Yeah? Well, I hope you know going to chapel every day don't make you a Christian, just like sleeping in a garage every day don't make you a car."

He laughs and tells me he's trying.

"Don't try," I tell him.

"I know, *DO*."

I tell Ike that everyone from the family is off drugs and going to church now. Then I tell him one of my favorite stories from *Chicken Soup for the Soul* and add a little West Side flavor in there.

"There was a little girl who took a long walk in the streets of Chicago. On her walk, she saw a mother and her child sitting on the ground with a sign that read, HUNGRY PLEASE GIVE. She saw gang members jumping a little innocent boy into a gang. She saw a mother and a father trying to trade in their food stamps for cash so they could get their drug fix.

"She saw a hooker getting smacked around by her pimp with nowhere for her to run. She saw people leaving a funeral that was the result of gang violence, while a brokenhearted family wept. She saw a young girl with a miniskirt hanging around with guys, looking for love in all the wrong places. She saw two brothers wearing backpacks get bullied by the local schoolkids while others stood by and laughed.

"She saw posters of missing kids on telephone poles, and young boys no more than thirteen in the back of police cars with their heads hanging down. Right there, she developed a burden and began to question God. As a tear rolled down her face, she said, 'God, if you are up there and if you are real, do you see all this madness? Do you see these hurting people, their pain, their tears? If you do, why don't you do something about this?' And God replied, 'I have already done something . . . I made you.'"

Ike smiles and nods his head. "I love that."

"My mom was real crazy out in the street, but now that she's saved she's like that little girl. She believes she's here to change the world. It's bigger than going to chapel, Ike. It's about what you do outside of chapel."

Ike tells me I'm a good kid and have always been his favorite. It feels good to talk to him like this, but I still plan to keep an eye on him.

The next day my family takes the bus to church together, and when we arrive the greeters are very happy to see us. They talk to Ike before service starts and I can tell that he feels comfortable. During praise and worship I see Ike lift his hands, and I'm shocked and can't stop staring.

When the preacher comes forth to speak, Ike gets up and tells us he is going to the restroom. The service goes on, but Ike doesn't come back. After a long time, one of the ushers comes to our row and asks my mom to step out for a second. I get nervous, wondering what could have happened. After a few minutes, my mom comes back to our seats and I give her a questioning look.

"Ike went to the coat rack and stole all the leather jackets."

My little brother Isaac laughs and says, "I knew it. I guess he won't be making it into the pearly gates!"

I tell him to shut up. "You okay, Mom?"

"I'm not, but God is in control."

I guess my conversation with Ike didn't go too far. I was trying to get him to understand that it's not just trying or wanting to change. I believe you have to make a choice, you have to decide. I make a choice right there and then that I am done with my old life. I choose rowing. I choose a future. I know it's easier to say I'll try than to do it. I haven't been institutionalized. Maybe if the judge saw Ike as his own son, he would have offered a therapist and some form of education instead of jail time. And things could have been different around here.

Winter training has been a beast, but I feel more confident every day. Rowing on the erg is the toughest workout I've ever done but I've learned to love it through patience and perseverance. Every time a friend at school thinks rowing is easy, I challenge them on the erg. When they're done, they have nothing but respect for the sport.

It works every part of my body at the same time. The sound of the fan tells me if I'm working hard or not. Even though I have nightmares about this damned machine killing me, I can see my body change every day because of it.

The team has spent the whole winter running the Manley staircase, erging, and strength training. I can breathe, think clearly, and finally touch my toes. I'm more focused than I've ever been. A couple of months ago, Coach Victor said to me, "What you once didn't know on the erg, you now know because of listening and practicing. You must enforce the same mentality in the classroom."

I'm doing better in my English classes because my teacher, Ms. Kris, makes us rap and sing out the definitions of words. She says, "If you can remember a song after listening to it three times, you can remember this stuff." She teaches the way we learn, and I find that after a heavy workout I'm more eager to learn than ever.

After class, I head down the stairs to meet Grace so I can walk her to the bus stop. I have good news to share and she's the first person I want to tell. When I see her I can't hold back and burst out, "I was chosen to compete in the cooking competition at Washburne Culinary & Hospitality Institute."

"That's awesome," she says, and gives me a hug. "What do you have to cook?"

"I have to do a knife skill test and cook four different egg dishes, some without using a spatula. Everything has to be perfect."

"I'm happy for you."

"Well, thank you," I say with a smile on my face. Being around Grace makes me want to succeed.

"Arshay, I have a name for you," Grace says. I tell her I want to hear it. "Molotti."

"Okay . . ." I say with a confused look.

"Molotti, Molotti, more head than body!"

I laugh. "You got jokes. You know you have a big head, too."

"I know, but yours is bigger!"

"Fine, Molotti it is."

As we walk, I debate about asking her on a real date. I know what makes her smile and what makes her sad. I know her favorite food, her secrets and her insecurities. I study her and listen to every word that comes out of her mouth. The walks are good, but I want to make sure that I don't get thrown into the friend zone. I know she has a wall up; I see countless guys try to talk to her and she waves them off. I have it bad for this girl and I want her to know.

I finally break the silence. "I want to take you out for dinner or a movie, like on a date."

She takes a deep breath. "I want to, but I'm still in love with Derrick and it's not fair to let you take me on a date when I still love someone else."

My heart is beating so hard, I feel like it's going to leap out of my chest. I don't know what to say. I just went from cloud nine to ground zero.

"I'm getting over it," Grace says. "Be patient with me."

"If there is anything I've learned over the years, it's patience," I tell her.

I just want to get to rowing practice at this point, so I tell her I'm late and we can catch up tomorrow. She whispers, "Don't be mad at me, Arshay."

"I'm not. I just need to get to practice."

"Okay, Molotti. Come to my place for dinner this week? I want you to meet my family."

I agree, knowing I must look like a sad puppy, and she says she will call me later.

Walking back to practice, I think hard about the bomb Grace just dropped on me. I figure that Grace needs a shoulder, an ear, a friend. Every guy around her wants something from her. The best thing I can give her is my shoulder and inspiration. My ego tells me to forget her and not to let her use me, but I think about a scripture my mom always says: "Don't grow weary in doing good, for you shall reap if you don't give up."

I'm late to practice again and Coach Jessica makes sure I know it before launching into a big announcement. "As most of you know, we will be going to Philadelphia for spring break."

"Are we going for the whole week, Coach Jessica?" Arthur asks.

"Yes, we are. We will be doing two a day, each day."

"Two what a day?" Malcolm asks with skepticism.

"Rowing practices."

"Oh hell naw, that's our vacation," Malcolm adds.

"You don't even know what a vacation looks like, Malcolm," Preston says.

"At least I know what my dad looks like, homie," Malcolm shoots back with rage.

Coach Jessica looks nervous. Usually, Coach Victor handles these altercations, but he is not in today. I want to be a leader and step in, but I'm not sure if they'll listen.

Preston says, "I'm gonna let this slide."

"I can do this all day, joe," Malcolm replies.

The room gets quiet. So far we've been doing everything right except getting along. We don't trust each other. I think, *this is Chicago.*

"Okay guys, chill out," Jessica says, taking a deep breath, face flaming red. "On the trip to Philly, we will practice twice a day on the water, do a couple of college visits and some sightseeing."

At that, the team starts to get hyped up.

"Also, this week everyone will take a swim test, and we will get in the boat for the first time."

We start clapping and yelling. She tells us that the coaches need to test us before choosing who is going to Philadelphia for spring break, and that she wants us to choose team captains today.

"Shouldn't we know if our captains can swim first?" Malcolm asks.

Before Coach can respond I say, "Arthur and Elliot." The gym goes quiet. "They are the two most mature guys. They don't clown around."

Arthur is a strong and sturdy senior with a reserved personality. He is a man of few words but when he talks, people listen. Elliot is a junior and is kind of a loner. I always see people teasing him because he has a Jheri curl perm and a box haircut. The jokes are mostly innocent but he is a nice guy and I feel bad for him. We've bonded because we both want to be chefs.

Coach Jessica looks around. "Is everyone okay with that?" Heads nod, except Malcolm's, but majority rules. I'm not sure anyone has earned the right to be captain yet, but if we have to pick it should be Arthur and Elliot. I learned at Victory Outreach that leadership is not the position, but the effort you put in. "Then, it's settled. Let's head to the YMCA and learn how to swim!"

I remember when I was younger, going to the local pool where the older guys forced us under water until we couldn't breathe. I stand in front of the pool at the YMCA now, with this memory running through my mind. I'm not too fond of water.

"Alright, those of you who can swim jump in! Everyone else watch what they do," Coach Victor yells. Alvin launches himself right into the deep end and swims like a fish. I'm surprised he can do anything besides beat the living crap out of someone.

The four girls on the team shrink away from Alvin's splash, saying they know how to swim but don't want to get their hair wet, and we laugh.

"You hoes don't know how to swim," Malcolm says. Coach Jessica shouts at Malcolm and the girls. I don't think anyone on the team really likes Malcolm.

Preston and Elliot also get in the water and the coaches realize no one else knows how to swim. They start working with us one-on-one. Alvin helps the coaches out by teaching some of the guys. Everyone is goofing off and throwing each other in the shallow end every time a coach turns their back.

I tentatively wade in and make my way over to Coach Victor. He shows me how to move my arms and asks me to swim from one end to the other. I start off at four feet. I pass five, six, and seven feet. People are clapping and cheering me on, but I'm starting to get nervous. I pass eight and nine. There is no way for my feet to touch and a wave of panic shoots through my body. I start to freak out and my arms move through the water wildly. Water is splashing my face and going in my mouth, and I start to go under. The lifeguard jumps in and pushes me over to the edge. I grab hold and catch my breath. I can hear everyone laughing, so I smile as if I'm fine, but I don't feel fine. I'm terrified. Most of us are.

Coach Jessica and Coach Victor look at each other as if to say this isn't what they signed up for, but they congratulate us and call it a day. In the locker room, the boys are slapping each other with towels and goofing off. Preston picks up Elliot's towel and makes a show of using it to dry off in between his legs. Malcolm's eyes go wide and the rest of the guys dissolve into laughter.

I walk over to a bench and sit down, too embarrassed to join in. My body is still shaking, and I can't stop thinking about the feeling of going under. I take a deep breath and tell myself that tonight I get to see Grace. That will make everything better.

I rush home from swim practice and quickly change to go to Grace's for dinner. When I arrive on the twenty-first block of Springfield, there are kids everywhere selling drugs, and they're all staring at me like I'm a three-legged monkey. It's one of the scariest corners I've ever seen, and I've seen scary. I'm a little nervous, because I know you can't just be a stranger walking into a neighborhood, chilling with girls from their block. That's a no-no. Also, taking the bus over is an even bigger problem, but I don't have a car.

She lives on a dead-end street next to the viaduct. If you cross over the viaduct, you are in the Mexican neighborhood. I say to myself, *I must love this girl, because I am going to die.* But when I get to the door and knock, she opens it with a warm smile and invites me in.

She introduces me to her mother, Karen, and her two little brothers. Right away I start playing with her little brother and his toy cars. I love kids, and he is the cutest thing. I talk to Karen about my classes, and brag about how I think her daughter is the smartest girl in school. Grace and I both live in single-parent homes and we understand what it's like. After dinner, Grace asks me if I have something for her.

"No, why?"

"What about the poem?"

I tell her it's going to be a long time before she gets that, I'm still working on it. I feel like as long as I am still working on it, she'll keep hanging out with me. I want to kiss her right there in her room but I know it's too soon. I have to understand that Derrick was her first and only and he isn't being straight with her about his feelings. I'm crazy about her, but I guess the waiting game continues.

I know she thinks she's being strong by holding on to him, but, as my aunt says, "You are stronger if you can let go." I want Grace to know what she's worth, and I promise her I will be patient with her in this process.

As I'm leaving her place, I say, "Wish me luck walking to the bus."

She laughs. "It's not so many gangbangers out."

"You wear glasses."

I kiss her on the forehead, thank her mother, and leave.

After school on Friday, we jump in a van and head to the Lincoln Park lagoon boathouse for our first day of rowing on the water. My fear is paralyzing me, and I can't shake the weak feeling in my arms and legs. My mind is playing tricks on me. I can hear voices in my head saying *open your eyes, you're not built for this. You don't even trust these people and you are going to get in the water with them? Remember what happened in the pool?*

We merge onto Lake Shore Drive. On my right, I see Navy Pier and on my left, behind me and in the distance, is the Sears Tower. It's amazing how beauty calms fear, like seeing Grace last night after struggling in the pool.

We pull up, and I'm looking directly at the back of the boathouse. After all our practicing, it is finally time to pick up an oar and get in a real boat. I can't believe we're here.

Ken meets us down at the boathouse and everyone is happy to see him. Some of the guys secretly call him the Cool Cracker. He is always telling us jokes and giving us words of inspiration, and you can tell his love for young people comes naturally. When I walk through the gate, my eyes go right to the boats as if they are resting on the same slings as on that day in the lunchroom.

Toward the dock, I see four slim young white dudes wearing tights putting their boat into the water. One looks directly at me and taps his buddy on the leg with a sly smirk. Malcolm rests his hand on my shoulder.

"They better not even think about asking us to wear those ass squeezers."

I laugh.

"It's all good, they told us to wear shorts and a T-shirt," I say.

"Yeah, but we gonna have to race in those."

"Not me," I reply.

Coach Jessica calls for us to bring it in around the boat.

"Hey, Coach Jessica, what do we wear in races?" Malcolm asks, looking surprisingly earnest.

"Well guys, for now, our preference is for you to continue practicing in fitted jersey shorts and a tank top or T-shirt. No cotton, it does not keep you warm if you get wet. No baggy clothes because it gets caught in the equipment. Stretchy is good. And for race day and future practice, we would like to get tank tops and spandex bottoms for you guys with Manley colors."

Everyone started going nuts, shouting, "We are not wearing those."

"Calm down," Ken says. "If you don't wear spandex, and your shorts get caught, it will cost you your race."

"Yeah, and if we wear those it will cost us our lives," Alvin says, laughing.

Jessica tells everyone we will talk about this later on and to get focused. She starts talking about the boat and our attention snaps to the sleek vessel in front of us. She explains each part we'll need to use, from the seats to the strapped-in shoes to the oarlocks. It's a lot to remember. She walks us through how to successfully take the boat off the slings and to the dock. The look on all the guys' faces makes me feel like I am on an episode of *The Twilight Zone*. Going on the water to row for the first time when you're from the hood is the scariest feeling in the world.

"Okay, guys, this is your time to shine. This is *your* moment," Coach Jessica says. We think we are big, bad, and tough, but try going out in the open water and putting your life in the hands of those who have no love for you.

Coach Jessica yells, "One mic; no one is talking while I am talking. Hands-on." Preston, Malcolm, Alvin, Arthur, Elliot, Deshaun, Danny, and I get hands-on.

"Up and over heads, and up." We barely get it up.

"When I say down to shoulders, split to the opposite side of riggers. Down to shoulders." *That feels much better*, I think to myself.

"Walk it to the dock, and walk." I can't believe we are walking toward the water.

As we get near the dock she yells, "Up and over heads, and up."

We strain under the boat's weight.

"One mic," Jessica demands.

We are now on the dock, and this shit is like watching-Stephen-King-movies-alone scary.

"Okay, toes to the edge." No one moves.

"I said toes to the edge of the dock." We move slowly to the edge.

"Down to waist." The boat lowers to our waists.

"Don't drop the boat, fools," Preston snaps.

"He always has something to say," Alvin whispers.

"Out and into the water, and down." The boat finally touches the surface of the water, and we let it go. We all start clapping, taking in our success.

A few of us head back to get the oars while a couple guys stay and hold the boat near the dock so it won't float away. The coaches show us how to put the oars in the oarlocks, and then it's finally time for us to get in the boat.

We are all a bit shaky.

"This boat is so skinny. How in the hell are we gonna get in here?" Danny asks, staring down at it. Coach Victor assures us we'll fit, and Elliot asks if we have to put our feet in the shoes and get locked in.

"What if the boat flips over?" I can tell he's trying not to let on how nervous he is.

Coach Jessica says we should trust her that the boat won't flip, but Malcolm blurts out, "Forget that," and walks back up to the boathouse. The coaches yell after him to get back down here, and ask where he's going.

"To get a life jacket," he yells back. All our heads pop up.

A mad rush for life jackets begins and the coaches are imploring us to return to the boat. Ken convinces the coaches to let everyone get life jackets if it makes them more comfortable. Elliot, Alvin, and I are the only ones who don't get them. It wasn't that I was confident in my swimming ability, but I wanted to stand out.

When it's time to get in the boat, I chide the others. "It's a shame that you guys live on blocks where there are stabbings, robberies, and drive-by shootings every day and yet you're scared to get in the water."

Malcolm asks why I'm not scared.

"I am. I'm also scared of shootings, but I still go outside."

"You think you so clever, Arshay," says Danny. I get the feeling he still doesn't like me, but I brush it off. I think he is only on the team to go to Philly.

"You will get in the boat in pairs because it's your first time. Usually, you will get in all eight at once."

"I'm good with that," I add, psyching myself up.

"Okay guys, in front of your seat is a white stripe on the board between the slide runner. You will place one foot on that while holding on to your oar, step in, and take a seat. Keep your foot there until you take a seat and then put your feet in the shoes. And never let go of your oar."

"Damn, joe, you have to be flexible for that," Danny says.

"Stern pair one, foot in and down," Coach Jessica calls. Malcolm and Preston climb in with visible uneasiness.

"Seat six and five, one foot in and down." Arthur and Elliot get in next. Then Danny and Deshaun, and now it's my turn. I grab the oar and step in after Coach Jessica gives the signal. My legs are vibrating, but I can't tell if it's from fear or instability or both. I drop my butt and hit the board. I am not on my seat, so Ken comes and holds me up and then slides my seat to where it should be. I place my feet in the shoes. My mind is blowing a fuse and all the coaches' careful instructions are gone. To top it off, Alvin is sitting behind me in the bow. I don't trust him as far as I can throw him.

"Count down from bow when ready," Coach Jessica instructs.

"Bow," Alvin yells.

"Bow," I scream.

"No, you are seat two, Arshay," she says.

"Two," I scream again.

Then everyone shouts their seat number until we hear "Stroke seat!" from Preston in the back.

"Okay, everyone sit tall like we learned on the erg. Hold your oars the way we taught you in the tanks, and trust your abilities like you did when you jumped in the pool." I grip the oars tighter as Coach Jessica speaks, remembering my training. She is sitting in the coxswain seat, and that makes me feel a tad relaxed.

Preston asks Coach Jessica how much the boat costs, in case we ruin it. "About thirty thousand dollars."

"Daaamn," says every kid in that boat.

"Okay, put your hands on the dock, and in two, we push away with some of those muscles you guys have—one two and shove." We hardly go anywhere. Ken comes up and grabs the blade of my oar.

"Arshay, push against me," he says and gives me a wink.

I push with everything I have and we glide out into open water. My triumph is immediately followed by fear as the boat starts to drift away. It's not even close to being balanced.

"Blades flat on the water and oars pressed against the oarlocks," Coach Jessica shouts.

"No, no, no, take me back in," Deshaun yells. His panic is contagious, and everyone starts freaking out. I see Malcolm's oar blades rising, and Jessica tells him to lift his hands. The boat tilts a bit more, and Deshaun cries, "Please, God. Please, God."

Coach Jessica tries to quiet us and instructs Alvin and me to row first, but we tell her we can't. We are too afraid. Everyone is complaining, some to the point of tears. To our relief, Ken tells Coach Jessica to bring it back in. I am just thankful that no other teams are on the water to witness this.

When we get off the boat, everyone starts teasing Deshaun for freaking out even though we all were. He doesn't care though, he is still a mess. The coaches look a little disappointed, but I don't know what they were expecting. This is all completely foreign to us. I want to tell Ken not to give up on us because we've been through a lot tougher, we will manage this with time.

Instead, I keep my thoughts to myself, and we put the boat away and walk to the van as if we just lost a race. Then I realize that at least now I have a good reason to call Grace tonight, and I'm at peace.

6

A Different World

Cooking dinner with Mom feels like Gospel Brunch Sundays. We have some Shirley Caesar playing, Mom is speaking in tongues, and everyone is talking over each other. We've started preparing healthy food since Ken told us about eating clean. It took a lot of convincing for my mom because black people love fried food.

Pamela walks into the kitchen, asking, "What's for dinner?"

"Baked chicken and boiled vegetables," I reply.

"I'm not eating that shit, I want fried chicken," Pamela whines. My little brother and sister hate when we eat healthily.

"Well, people in hell want a cup of ice water, it doesn't mean they get it. So, don't eat," I reply.

"Boy bye, I'm starving."

"If you are not going to eat this baked chicken, you're not starving. You just want something better."

Mom runs out of patience and tells Pamela to leave the kitchen and read her Bible. Momma always gives us room to make mistakes, but Pamela tries my mom's patience almost every day. Since my mom's big change, she doesn't hit us anymore. If she comes close Pamela says, "Go ahead and beat us, be who you used to be." That stops her in her tracks.

Pamela's always had a dirty mouth, which my mom tried to put a stop to before she went into the home by washing her mouth out with soap every time she cursed. It was painful to watch. She knows my mom won't do that now, so she takes advantage. Although my mom doesn't hit us, she will put us on something called *discipline*, a punishment she learned in the recovery home. It includes things like scrubbing walls with a towel, washing a neighbor's car, or cleaning our siblings' shoes with a toothbrush. I can't stand *discipline*, but it does lessen the fighting in our home.

We only cook for four now. Shaundell's still camping out at my grandmother's. Ike came back after stealing those leather jackets from the church saying he'd change, but he didn't, of course, and Mom finally gave him the boot.

I take the chicken out of the oven and walk to the front room for some air. As I get close to the door, I hear the knob start to turn and I freak out, rushing toward it to hold it shut, thinking that it's the drug addict zombies. Before I get to the door, it pushes open and I pray silently that it's Shaundell. The door swings open wider and I see that it's not my brother, but Ken from rowing. My heart is pounding. Why is he here?

"What's up, Arshay?" Ken asks casually. He is with the female athletic director from the school, Coach Jones.

"Dude, you can't just be walking in black folks' house! What's wrong with you?"

"I have to meet all the parents before the Philadelphia trip," he explains, looking confused.

"Hold on, I'll ask my mom to come out to the door," I tell him, shaking my head. We never have company, and I don't want Ken to see that we live in a one-bedroom apartment. I yell for my mom to come to the door.

"Mom, this is Coach Ken."

She looks at me. "From the boat thing?"

"Yes, Mom, the rowing team."

I haven't told my mom about Philadelphia yet. I planned to wait until the last minute so she couldn't say no. I head into the kitchen to finish cooking the vegetables while my mom talks to Ken and Coach Jones. After they finish talking, I say goodbye and my mom closes the door behind them.

"Why didn't you tell me about Philly?"

I laugh. "I didn't want you to come up with any bright ideas, like I can go but I'll have to join the church choir or something."

She smiles. "That coach of yours seems like a really nice guy."

"He is one of a kind."

"Seems like it's going to be an experience."

"Yeah, if we can learn not to be afraid of water."

She laughs at that, but then her eyes get serious. "Arshay, I have to tell you something. When you graduated from the eighth grade I had a vision. I have never had one like this before, Arshay. Something inside me knew that you would be great, that you would go places that no one in this community would ever think to go, that you would be in the presence of kings."

I am blown away, but part of me thinks she's trippin'. The people at church call her the Prayer Warrior because of her visions, but when it comes to predicting my future, I'm not so sure.

After school the next day, I tell the team how Ken just opened my door and tried to walk into my apartment.

"Hell yeah, man," Alvin tells us, "this dude knocked on my door, too. I answered and told him to wait a second; I'm going to get my dad. I walked to the kitchen and my dad had a look on his face like he's going to kill someone. I turned around, and Ken is right behind me. My dad doesn't play like that, man, he don't even like white people."

Preston joins in. "My sister was yelling that the police were at the door!"

Everyone has a similar story. I'm surprised he didn't get himself killed, but it's pretty funny hearing talk about Ken just walking into their homes without permission.

"You guys don't call him the Cool Cracker for nothing," I tell the team, and everyone starts laughing.

There are a few days left of school before spring break, and everyone is excited and nervous. I promised myself I'd ask Grace what's going on with us before the trip to Philly. I can't wait around for her to decide whether she wants me or not, but there's also another girl, Tiffany, who lives on my block. She told me she actually likes me. I don't know why, but a year ago I told Tiffany I didn't want to date her, have sex with her, or even dream about her. I said I just wanted to play cards, laugh, and debate as friends. I was a little firm, but she hung in there until I matured.

I can't give Tiffany my heart right now because my heart is still with Grace. Which must be the same thing that's happening with Grace and me. She is interested in me but still waiting on an answer from Derrick, I guess. I always tell myself how dumb it is to wait on someone like this, but I'm still young and willing to put in the time. If I'm going to do that, at least it's with the smartest girl in our class and no one else.

When Grace and I are walking to the bus stop later, I decide to ask her.

"Are you done with Derrick? I need to know because I really like you. I love our friendship, but I like you." I should stop talking but I continue, "There is kind of this girl that likes me—"

"It's okay. I don't expect you to wait. You should try to make it happen with that girl." My body goes numb and my hearing goes out for a second. I am pretty sure I just died and came back.

"No, but I'm not really into her. I am just saying . . ."

"I'll tell you what; I will give you an answer for sure *after* spring break."

"Deal."

I will never understand why the ones we like don't like us back, or why we're never interested in the ones who actually do like us.

Listening to my mom's scripture readings, I've learned how love is supposed to be: gentle, kind, not boastful, not jealous, not irritable, not self-seeking, not easily angered. It keeps no record of wrong, never gives up, always protects, always trusts, and is always hopeful. I know that I need to practice having patience, especially when it comes to Grace. Patience has shown me some of Grace's strengths, strong aspects of her personality that I probably wouldn't have seen if I was actually with her. I've also seen her weaknesses, and patience gave me the opportunity to know what I can and cannot deal with before investing more time. I am starting to realize that if you don't take the time to get to know a person first, you will only waste time, and it may lead to an unplanned baby, a divorce, or a painful breakup. All things considered, waiting on Grace seems like the best step.

I am buzzing with excitement as I walk to school from the Blue Line train. It's a beautiful Saturday, and finally time for the team to go to Philadelphia. In the school parking lot, I see a huge white bus with *$7,000* written on the window. You can tell it's an old yellow school bus that someone painted white; they did a horrible job. I immediately name it the Marshmallow Man. Ken is there with Coach Jessica and Coach Victor as the other students arrive. I ask Ken if he's driving with us, and he tells me he isn't but to make sure we behave.

When I get on the bus, Malcolm is sitting in the back next to a skinny kid with glasses.

"Hey, Malcolm, who is this guy? I never saw him before."

"This is my nephew, Pookie. He's visiting from Germany."

"He's your nephew?" I ask him. "He's your age."

"He's my sister's son, fool."

"Ken said he can go?" I ask.

"Yeah, Ken already talked to my Old G, now mind your business," Malcolm says. Sometimes things here seem a bit unorganized but what do I know.

I laugh and nod at Pookie, and he shakes my hand and nods. I think Pookie is a little weird, or maybe just shy.

When I walk off the bus to say hello to everyone, I see a very short Puerto Rican woman. She has a mole on the right side of her face, baggy blue jeans, and a black leather jacket. She tells me in a thick accent that she's Lupe, the bus driver. I want to laugh because she popped up out of nowhere and she's swinging a big Jheri curl in my face. I say hello back just as Alvin pulls up with his father, a tall, dark, and scary-looking man. He kind of reminds me of the cook from *A Different World*. Alvin's brother, who is known as Pooh Trigga, is a senior at Manley and is coming with us as well. They both seem to get their toughness from their father. To my surprise, I see them shake hands with Pheodus. Pheodus is about six feet tall and has muscles on top of muscles. He wears baggy clothes and has the most beautiful nappy hair you will ever see. He is known for being a loner. Maybe being on the crew team will win him some friends.

Once all nineteen students have arrived—fifteen boys and four girls—Ken asks everyone to get on the bus. Everyone kisses their families good-bye.

"Okay," Ken says, looking out over all of us, "I want you guys to have fun. I only have three rules: no baby making, no fighting, and listen to your coaches."

"Got it," we say back.

"Have fun, and see you there."

Coach Victor tells us to raise our hand when he says our name. "Arshay, Malcolm, Anthony"—who is Pookie—"Preston, Leslie, Leah, Terry, Antwon, Tavares, Deshaun, Ronald, Alvin, Arthur, Sabrina"—a friend who came along with Leah—"Tanika, Marcus, Pheodus, Elliot, Danny."

We are all accounted for. I guess Pooh Trigga's real name is Tavares.

"Okay, guys, this is our training camp. Let's see who can make it past this, and then we're on our way to history!" We start clapping and shouting. I'm not sure if this is going to be a disaster or a success, but time will tell.

The trip to Philadelphia has been quiet because no one really knows each other and this group has a few different cliques. About halfway to Philly, everyone starts complaining about their backs hurting because of the hard seats. It is pretty painful; I don't think school-bus seats are meant to be sat on for more than a few hours. Coach Victor tells us to stop complaining since none of us are paying for anything.

About eight hours into the trip we start singing songs and creating chants. A few of the guys get bored and put Vaseline up the noses of the guys that are asleep. They wake up angry but no one will tell who did it. Other than that, the ride is pretty smooth. At one point, I head to the back of the bus to talk to Uncle Malcolm and Pookie. I ask Pookie what it's like to live in Germany. He says it's okay, but in a low, weird voice. I'm intrigued because I've never met anyone who lived in another country. He tells me that his dad is in the army and his mom is a nurse. I ask him about a thousand more questions and I can tell he is getting a little annoyed.

Finally, he says, "Dude, I live in Chicago. I don't live in no damn Germany. I just wanted to go to Philly with Malcolm."

I just back up and put my hands up. "My bad."

"It's all good, but Malcolm *is* my uncle." I walk away, telling him to enjoy the trip.

I wake up to the city lights of downtown Philadelphia, the home of brotherly love. It's late, and I can't see the vibrant parks that a church friend mentioned, but what I do see has every awakened person strolling on the bus in full-blown reverence. We see more museums than people. Across the river from the expressway is Boathouse Row. It is a strand of different boat clubs, side by side, decorated with Christmas lights and the Mecca of Philly rowing where we will be tomorrow. I wish I could tell you I dreamed of this. I am content with our one-bedroom, sober mom, and crushing on Grace. But inside my heart of hearts, I know there is more. I'm not sure if I am just thrilled to be somewhere else, but to me, this city carries the joy of a thousand ice-cream trucks, and I haven't been here for a half hour.

Soon we pull up slowly to a large house in the middle of the woods.

As everyone wakes up, Malcolm shouts, "See! I knew they is going to kill us niggas out here."

Preston yells at him to shut up, but sounds nervous. Coach Victor and Jessica tell us we are here, and to get our things together.

We get off the bus and walk into the most beautiful house I have ever seen. It is the size of a mini museum and stars blanket the sky. Ken greets us all at the door and introduces us to his friends Ted and Tracy, who own the house. They are a lovely white couple with big smiles, and you can see their huge hearts beaming from their faces. They shake everyone's hand and show us around. Before we can put our bags down, everyone starts running around claiming rooms. Ken tells us he wants us all to get some rest.

"It's late, and tomorrow we are going sightseeing and Monday we will get right to work."

Ken goes into Ted and Tracy's room and they shut the door. We go into rooms in groups of four; Preston, Malcolm, and Pookie are in a room with me. Malcolm tells us that something isn't right that Ken is in the room with Ted and his wife.

"What's not right, Malcolm? They're friends," I tell him.

Malcolm is lying down staring at the ceiling. "White people be on some freaky stuff."

We laugh, and Malcolm says he's going to listen at the door.

"Y'all coming?"

"No, go have fun," the rest of us tell him. He leaves the room.

I ask Pookie what's wrong with his uncle, and Pookie tells me he's been trying to figure him out for years.

I talk myself to sleep. I wake up an hour later to laughing and feel shaving cream on my face and a teddy bear in my arms.

"Real nice, guys."

Now that I'm awake, I go into the other rooms. There are another half-dozen people asleep with shaving cream on their faces. I know right away that it's Malcolm and Preston. When I see Preston he tells me he wants to throw Alvin's shoes in the woods because his feet smell.

"No man, that's going to be a fight," I tell him.

"He won't know it's us."

"Because it's not going to be us."

"Whateva." He grabs Alvin's shoes and tiptoes out to the second-floor deck and tosses them into the tree line. *It's going to be a long week.*

The next morning there are fruit, bagels, and cream cheese on the table. Everyone begins complaining, asking where the donuts and cereal are. Ken has another talk with us about nutrition. I go into the kitchen and check out the stove. It is a nice stainless-steel stove and I am in love with it. Ken walks in and sees me eyeing the hardware.

"You like that?"

"Yep."

"How is cooking class?"

"I got 92 out of 100 in a competition they had at Washburn College, but there were a lot better scores."

"That's good. Just keep working at it," Ken tells me, opening the refrigerator. "The nights that we have dinner here, I would love for you to be in charge of cooking. Are you okay with that?"

"I'm okay with that. I'm just grateful to be here."

He tells me to put together a grocery list and he will go to the store for me later. I feel honored to cook for everyone and to show what I've learned in the last year.

We spend the whole day sightseeing and checking out sights like Independence National Historical Park and the Liberty Bell. Preston asks if we can run up the Rocky stairs. Ken says we will, later in the week. When we get back to the house after sightseeing, Ken and the coaches explain the next few days to us. We are all nervous but excited to get out onto the water.

I barbecue some chicken and pork chops for dinner and it's a huge success. I notice Arthur's sister, Leah, has her eye on me. She recently joined the team, and I think she likes that I can cook a good meal, but I don't need another cutie in my life. She is thin and pretty with full lips. She has long braids that go down to her back. I tell Preston that Leah has been watching me.

"You in trouble." He laughs.

"That's what I said!"

I feel like there is no room in my heart for another girl, though I don't think there's anything wrong with flirting.

I head into the front room where Alvin is playing cards with his brother, Terry; Danny; Elliot; and Pheodus. They are playing deuces wild for dollar bills. Everyone is pissed because they have lost most of their money to either Alvin or Pooh Trigga. They seem to be very good at playing cards, and they tell us they've been playing that game for years. I notice that everyone seems to be getting to know one another better, but there are still some cliques in the group.

In the morning, we rise quickly and head to the University of Pennsylvania cafeteria. We step off the bus at Penn and onto the bronze and gray brick ground, and I think to myself, this must be what it feels like to be surrounded by castles. The feel is almost identical to the University of Wisconsin, but the students are more diverse. By the look of what everyone is wearing, the campus must be judgment-free. I'm afraid I can't say

I know what that feels like. I instantly fall in love with the chestnut color of the school and the engraving of history quotes everywhere. As I walk behind the Manley Crew team as they head to the cafeteria, I stop to take a deep breath. The nineteen of them are walking on sunshine as I watch them. I think to myself that this rowing thing might very well work out.

I can't believe it when I find out it's all you can eat. We're blown away by the sight of the beautiful college girls, so we split up and sit next to them. They can tell we are high school students, even though we try to say we are in college. We have seconds and thirds for breakfast, and I am in love with college. It reminds me of the television show *A Different World*. Watching that show inspired me to think about college for the first time, and now I'm getting the opportunity to live it.

After breakfast, we take the Marshmallow Man over to the Penn boathouse. Malcolm tells us that Lupe has been drinking liquor out of her coffee cup.

"Shut up, Malcolm," we say in unison.

The boathouse is a beautiful brown, red, and blue, with the smell of hard work and water. There are boats everywhere, and they are being polished like brand-new Ferraris.

"Okay, guys, this is where I rowed," Ken tells us. "This is home to me. Respect everyone you see and let's have a good workout and work hard. Now go upstairs to the locker room and get changed."

We are amazed by the pictures on the wall, the workout room, and the crew shirts we see. The boathouse is full of tradition. I am so pumped and ready to go. Ken warms us up by taking us to run the hills across the street from the boathouse. Terry, the most overweight of our teammates, is all the way in back for the entire run. He is yelling that he can't do it, so Ken goes and runs by his side, motivating him and pushing him the whole time. Ken talks to Terry about believing in himself, and tells him that by the end of the week he will not be last. Ken asks a few of us to continue to push Terry, even though we are pretty exhausted. Some of us have never run hills before, and we're still out of shape.

When we get back to the boathouse, it's time to row. We all are rocking basketball shorts and T-shirts. There is still no mention of uniforms yet. I feel like we're all so embarrassed from the last time we rowed that we are ready to erase that memory. Some of the guys are still making fun of Deshaun for crying on the boat. He says it's a conspiracy. Coach Jessica reminds us how to carry the boat. Some of the guys complain that the others aren't really holding their weight. When we get to the water, we lift the boat over our heads and grab the inside, then slowly place the boat into the water. This time it is much smoother.

After testing out our erg machine skills, they pick the best eight to be the first to row: Malcolm, Preston, Arthur, Elliot, Antwon, Ronald, Alvin, and me.

"That's some bull," Pooh Trigga says. "I don't want to be on the scrub team."

Coach Jessica calms him down, saying, "You're not a scrub. Some of these guys will be on that boat, too. Ken will do some workouts with you guys while we row." Alvin is disappointed after hearing his brother Pooh Trigga is not in our eight; his mood has downright changed.

We get on the boat again in twos and push off. Calling the shots from a small motor boat and a bullhorn is Mike O'Gorman, a former Penn crew team member and an employee of Alpart Trading. He is the guy that Ken told us about who gave him the idea to start this team. He's here to help with the coaching for a few days. Mike has won numerous national championships as a coach, and he's also won medals in world championships as a coxswain. He's a short white guy with big curly hair and looks like Booger from *Revenge of the Nerds*. He starts with a couple of jokes that we don't understand, but he certainly cracks himself up. He remembers all of our names right away. From the bullhorn he says, "Bow two," which is me and Alvin, "I want you to go forward all the way up to the catch, and when I say 'row,' I want you to drive the blade into the water and row just like you did in the tank and on the erg."

Mike signals and we reach all the way forward. Our blades are sticking out of the water and pointing skyward while the other team members' blades rest on the water.

"Okay, make sure you row in sync. Alvin, follow Arshay. Ready . . . set . . . row!"

It's all moving so fast, but we drop our oars in the water and push off and we are rowing! I can't believe I am in open water rowing in the City of Brotherly Love. But are both talking over each other while trying to figure out how to sync our oars.

"Okay, in two rows I will say 'way enough' and I want you to stop and rest your blades in the water," Mike says, and we do it without any mistakes. He does the same technique with all the other pairs in the boat. He is a great teacher; he easily explains everything using different metaphors.

"Okay, now the stern pair," Mike says to Preston and Malcolm, "seat seven and eight. I want you guys to go up to the catch. The stern pair is responsible for setting the rhythm for the rest of the boat to follow. When I say 'row' I want you to row and slowly the other pairs will join in."

We're all shouting that we aren't ready for that, but Mike wants to try anyway. Alvin whispers from the back, "This cracker is trying to kill us out here," and I start laughing.

"Ready . . . set . . . row!" Mike screams, and we start rowing again, "Okay, in two, seat five and six join in. You guys are called the stern four. One, two, *go!*"

The other guys join in a little late and the boat begins jerking and we start screaming every curse word in the book. The timing is off. Mike screams "way enough" and he tells us we're going to start over, so we start again. He asks that this time we follow his voice.

"Stern pair to the catch, now row! In two, seat five and six!" he shouts, "One, two, and row!"

They start rowing and the boat is gliding. It is a great feeling and you can tell that we are all giddy. After several tries, seats three and four join in, and we are really zooming.

Mike has us try adding in the last two seats, but I don't go at the right time. The boat starts listing again. We see a team row past us giggling, and hear one guy say, "They have life jackets on." Coach Jessica, who is in the coxswain seat, tells us not to mind them, they're jerks. Mike tells us the good news is that we are really strong and just need to work on our technique. We see another team pass and they look so smooth, rowing past us so peacefully. I notice that their blades come out of the water facing upward, turn parallel to the water coming back toward the catch, and then drop back in the water facing upward. It looks effortlessly fluid. We ask Coach Jessica what that's called, and why we aren't doing it. She says it's called "feathering." She says that in a feathered position, the oar blade meets with less wind resistance. Less wind resistance means a faster stroke.

"You guys will learn that soon, now it's not important."

I am happy to wait. We spend an hour rowing and working on our technique and then pull into the dock. Four other students get into the boat. Coach Jessica keeps Alvin, Preston, Malcolm, and me on the boat; I'm excited because I am eager to learn more.

After our day of rowing, Ken tells us to go into the boathouse to shower. When we run upstairs, we see that it's a community style shower. After some complaining about having to shower together, and some corny jokes from Mike O'Gorman, we get on the Marshmallow Man heading for a Penn campus tour. We talk about our rowing experience on the bus the whole time. We agree that it is one of the hardest things we've ever done.

"To get eight guys to do the same exact thing, all at one time, and at such a fast pace with every part of your body is insane," Arthur says.

I sit up on my seat. "Agreed. You play basketball, you can play soccer, play baseball, hell, even sometimes play fight, but you can't play rowing, it's brutal. We can dance, run, throw, shoot, fight, kick, but rowing is foreign for us."

Coach Victor tells us that the odds are against us.

"But I'm telling you guys, we are really on to something here. I don't think there has ever been another crew of eight black men that have done this all together before, so you may very well be the first."

When we arrive at the campus there is a huge rally going on. People are passing out flyers for various causes. Alvin asks for the team video camera and starts going up to people, asking about their thoughts on the possibility of a black rowing team. Some people laugh, some people say it would be awesome, and some think that people would never take it seriously.

Everyone walking around Penn campus seems to be cool, serious, and smart. After walking around awhile, we go into the W. E. B. Du Bois College House. Most of the programs and events in the Du Bois House are based on the history and culture of the people of the African diaspora. There are five black students there to show us around, give us some history, and talk to us about college life as an African American at Penn.

Toward the end of the day, we have a group discussion about gender, diversity, and education. This starts some pretty heated debates between Malcolm and Leah. After a discussion on race, Malcolm raises his hand to say, "It's hard to forgive a group of folks who spread crack in our communities to destroy our families and used acid to kill their own."

"Nobody forces them to smoke it, Malcolm," Leah says.

"Yeah, but people were losing their kids due to racism, and this was the only thing they were giving to them to be able not to feel anymore. Or a Bible." I instantly start thinking about my grandfather, who turned to drugs to cope with racism, and I thought about my mom, who turned to drugs to cope with him.

"Malcolm, you just hate white people," Leah says.

"I come from a family of Muslims, and you can't mistake our pro blackness for hate."

The whole class blows up yelling. The facilitator calms everyone down and does an exercise that challenges us to step out and learn more about ourselves, the community, and those who don't look like us. I think about Ken, Coach Jessica, the Mexican pastor from Victory Outreach, and my mom's message of love to the streets. And my observation is this: It's going to take a whole village to change the West Side. I'm happy to learn about the diversity and power we could have if everyone came together. Although W. E. B. Du Bois is an African American–themed college house, it is one of the most diverse spots on campus. The students help us realize how important high school is if we want to get accepted to a good college.

On the way home I sit next to Alvin on the Marshmallow Man. I saw him really listening and tuned in to what our student guides were talking about, so I ask him why he's in the gangs.

"I'm not a gang member, and I see the way you look at me, man. Judging and all. When we first moved to the West Side, I was walking with my brother Rob. And some guys were going to jump us. So, I told Rob to run and get Dad, and he flew. They rushed me, and I picked up bottles and sticks and threw them like no tomorrow. They got a few hits in, but they saw how crazy I got and bolted. Then this guy name Spot Man walked from across the street and told me he wanted to help but he couldn't because he didn't know me. Then he guarantees me that this will happen again, and if my brothers wanted protection, we would have to hang with them. And guess what I choose?"

"Protection," I say.

"I had no choice," he replies.

"I grew up with those guys. It's a rule if someone from your hood gets jumped, you help them. If not, you get jumped." He keeps his head down as he talks. "I feel bad for every guy we beat up. That's not really me. But if I want to be protected, I have to help. We go to a school with too many gangs. Who is going to help you if you get jumped?"

"I guess . . . Preston?"

"Yeah, but that's it."

"I understand where you coming from, but it doesn't have to be that way," I tell Alvin. "If I am walking on campus today and you bump me, at that second I am in control of the situation, not you. I have the choice to react like a hard tough dude from the West Side or a smart young black man that knows that I'm responsible for my actions. Whatever I do decides the outcome. And for the record, you have been hanging with us for months now and not them. You have a choice, and made it. The team got your back, man."

He looks at me sideways. "You some kind of preacher or something?"

"No." I laugh. "But I've learned a lot from the youth service and the guys at my mom's church. You should come sometime. It's not a robe wearing, people screaming, money asking kind of church."

"Most people at church are phony."

"Most people on this bus are phony, and our school, and homes. We still go there."

"Right, but did you know I never get into a fight because of me? Every fight I've been in is because of my brother, or my sister, or my friends. I don't like trouble, it just follows me."

"It follows me, too, Alvin, but I'm fast as hell and I can run." We both start laughing, and I ask Alvin why his brother is called Pooh Trigga.

"He is really just Pooh, but it sounded too soft so we put the 'Trigga' behind it."

I nod, laughing, and tell him I have one more question.

"How do you and Pooh Trigga win the card games?"

"Don't say anything, but we cheat. We just let each other know what we get."

"That's cold," I tell him, and now we're both laughing.

When we get back to Ted and Tracy's house, Ken urges us to shower and tells us he's taking us somewhere cool for dinner. We get dressed and back on the bus as fast as possible. We pull up to another big house in the middle of the woods and find out it's a house owned by one of Coach Jessica's friends. They are hosting a party for us. Inside is a big table full of food, a party room that looks like a casino, and some very happy country folks. We feel welcome right away.

Ken tells us to turn on some hip-hop and we run to the stereo to find tunes.

"Ken, what you know about this music?" says Marcus as he takes Sabrina to the dance floor. Marcus is tall and slim of build, which is good for rowing, but I don't think he is into it long term. He's focusing on graduating and that's all he talks about. He dates Leah's best friend, a sophomore. We figure he only came on the trip to keep an eye on her.

We have a great time and dance all night. When it's time to go, we can't leave because Lupe is passed out drunk. Hours pass and we chill and watch movies until she is sobered up.

We're scared on our way home because it's so dark, but Lupe has it under control. I'm sure she's been in this situation many times before.

The rest of the week is strictly training every day. Our morning routine is breakfast on campus, running hills, two hours of boat time, a school visit, and back to practice on the erg machines. Ken is usually the cool one that we love, but when it comes to training he is very serious. He pushes all of us way past our limits, even though we complain most of the time. He is really into helping Terry, and I notice he's shed a couple pounds. With the help of Mike O'Gorman, we learn to row together. It takes a few days, but eventually we catch on. It is a tough week. Moving that boat with all of our strength for more than one minute requires us to be in top shape, but when we finally get it we feel incredible. We still see the other rowers looking at us as if we are flying dogs, but we know that it's new to their eyes and will take some getting used to. The life jackets aren't helping, either. I learn a lot at Victory Outreach church about being a young leader and team player. This week, I have gotten a sense of what being a teammate is all about. More than any other sport, rowing instills discipline and skill that you can only obtain by spending hours of beating your craft. Unlike ball sports, there are no superstars. Just eight rowers that have to move in the same exact way at the same time to push the boat forward. Ken was right; it's not all about athletic abilities but work ethic. What you put in is what you get out. At the Penn Boathouse, these college rowers are on the

Ted's friends gives me twenty bucks for having the courage to recite my poem. "That's good writing."

That is the second poem I wrote before starting Grace's. My inspiration came from watching *The Fresh Prince* and *Family Matters*. The people on those shows look just like me but have totally different lives. Life is sweet for the black families on television. They have family dinner together every night, the kids get an allowance every weekend, the big brother and sister go to college, and when the kids make a mistake or struggle, the parents sit them down to correct them with love. Those television shows are like my personal church service and they give me hope. I want that life so badly. That's why I started writing "AM I."

After the talent show, I am talking to Ted when I hear screaming and banging out back. When we get outside, I realize Alvin is on the bus with Marcus's girl Sabrina, and Marcus is banging on the windows and doors. Marcus's friends on the team, Arthur and Antwon, are grabbing him, trying to calm him down and telling him he doesn't need any trouble with Alvin. Marcus walks away, smashing and kicking everything in sight.

"I can't believe this." You can hear the hurt in his voice.

Pooh Trigga comes running outside and yells at Alvin to come off the bus.

Ken asks what happened as Alvin steps out of the bus.

"Nothing, I was on the bus messing around with this chick."

"You know that Marcus is with her, what do you mean 'nothing'?"

Ken tells Alvin to take a walk with him, and I feel ashamed that Ted and his family has to witness this. Everyone is stirring up drama. I ask them, one by one, to chill out and just enjoy the rest of the night. I think everyone making it a big deal is scaring Ted's family.

Coach Victor is really pissed.

"We have to stop trying to kill each other; it's embarrassing. Black folks don't know how bad this looks."

I don't know how to respond to him, I feel like there is nothing I can do. For the first time on this trip, everyone is divided and goes their separate ways in the house. When Ken and Alvin come back, Alvin goes upstairs. I find Ken to talk to him.

"We have to keep Alvin on the team. He is good, we need him."

"Okay," Ken tells me, "but you have to be your brother's keeper."

"I can handle that."

When I go upstairs, Alvin, Pooh Trigga, Preston, Malcolm, Ronald, and Pookie are in the room. Some of them are plotting going over to the next room and smashing Arthur, Marcus, Elliot, and Antwon.

"You guys are crazy," I tell them. "Tell me what happened."

"I was talking to her, we start kissing, and I tell her to meet me on the bus in five minutes. So I tell Pookie to look out for me and if someone comes, just throw something at the bus. Next thing you know, Marcus is trying to get on the bus and I had to bar the door." Everyone is laughing.

"I was throwing Skittles," Pookie pleads.

"Skittles? Who is going to hear that?"

Pooh Trigga says we should wait until we get back home to start something, but I tell them to squash it, they are all scared over there. I tell the guys that we need to go down and thank the people who hosted us, so that's what we do.

We leave in the morning, and it's a quiet ride. No one says much. I sit next to Leah and we laugh and joke the whole time; I can see that her brother is keeping his eye on us.

Every hour, Malcolm yells out to Lupe. "You're not drinking, right?"

"No, no, honey," she tells him with her thick accent.

I like Leah and she likes me, and I think I could just have fun with her while I wait for Grace to decide. Leah dated Arthur's best friend, so I figure she wants to do the same. After thinking about it for a few minutes, I realize I would only be wasting precious high school days. No matter what, those arrangements never end well; someone gets hurt. Above all things, Grace is the center of my heart.

. . .

Halfway through the trip home, everyone is complaining about their backs again. Malcolm starts cracking jokes on everybody one by one. "Pooh Trigga breath humming like a teapot on this bus." Everyone starts laughing.

"Arshay, why are you laughing?" he says. My heart drops. "Y'all know Arshay has the safest sex on the bus. No sex." People start cracking up.

"Marcus, where your girl?" Malcolm says, looking into his eyes. The whole bus gets quiet. Malcolm shouts, "Boy, she exposes you like dog nuts." Everyone jumps up, bursting with laughter. Marcus jumps up and gets in Malcolm's face. "Sit down now!" Lupe screams. Malcolm picks Marcus up by his neck and says, "What are you gonna do?" Marcus can't do anything. Even though Malcolm is only a freshman, he's strong. Coach Victor yells for Lupe to stop the bus, and she pulls over so fast that everyone is thrown into the back of the seat in front of them. Coach Victor tells Malcolm to get off the bus.

"But—he got in my face."

"Now!" Coach Victor screams, and we sit quietly while Malcolm walks off the bus.

Marcus sits back, upset, and screams at Sabrina, "You done this." She is crying and doesn't look back. When Malcolm gets back on the bus, he sits in front with Coach Victor. After all of this I have no idea what is going to happen to the team. Everything we've learned seems like it has gone out the door.

Pooh Trigga claims he has to use the bathroom bad and Lupe refuses.

"I'm not stopping. Pee in a bottle."

He finds an empty bottle. Pooh decides to dump the pee out the window while Lupe is driving eighty miles an hour. The pee flies right back into the bus on everyone through the windows. Everybody jumps up screaming as Lupe starts swerving, rushing to the rest stop. I can't believe this trip. The rest of the way home, no one says a word.

7

Alvin

A few days after the trip, I realize that I don't know if there is still a team. I think Malcolm might get kicked off, that a lot of people might quit, or that Ken and the coaches are going to give up on us. During our morning prayers at home I rarely ask to pray for anything, but today I ask my mom to pray for my team: for direction, unity, and for us to learn to believe. I don't fully understand how prayers work, but I do know that when my mom prays things happen in her favor.

I leave home early and get on the Blue Line train to O'Hare, departing at the Kedzie-Homan stop. I walk a few blocks south to Lexington Street. There are young guys already out hustling on the block; they stare me down like I don't belong. There are vacant lots and beer bottles everywhere. I arrive at West Lexington Street and a big pink building. I walk up the stairs feeling a little jittery. I ring the doorbell that says ROSS. It's about 7:30 a.m. I ring five times until I hear a girl's voice say hello.

"Is Alvin there?" I ask.

"Who is this?"

"It's Arshay. I'm on the team with Alvin and Pooh Trigga. I-I mean

Tavares." I hear a laugh, and she says I can come up. When I get upstairs, holding open the door is a cute girl with beautiful white teeth.

"Hey, I'm Angie, Alvin's sister. He's in back."

I walk to the back, past the kitchen, and see Alvin lying in bed asleep with Pooh Trigga and his younger brother Robert, who he talked about a little on the trip. I'm happy to see we aren't the only family that piles up in one bed to sleep.

"Alvin, wake up."

He looks up, surprised. "Boy, what the hell you doing here?"

"To wake you up for school so we can go together," I tell him.

"Alright, give me a second."

Pooh Trigga mumbles something about how this is some "gay stuff," but I don't respond. I wait in the kitchen. On the refrigerator, I notice there is a chain wrapped around it and locked. I try to open the refrigerator to see if I can get in.

"Boy, whatchu doing?" Alvin asks. I jump back a little.

"Dude, why is the refrigerator locked down?"

He laughs and tells me that if there isn't any food, he and his brothers will actually go to school instead of stay home and starve. I nod and ask him where the rest of his family is.

"My mom doesn't live here, and my dad is at work. He leaves early to drive trucks."

On our way downstairs I tell him I met his sister, and I think she's nice.

"You get your face kicked in if you touch my sister."

"You don't have to worry about that."

"Why did you come to my crib?" Alvin asked.

"I told Ken I will be my brother's keeper."

"Man, Ken's just lucky I'm not going to push Marcus's head back."

"That sounds painful, don't do that." We both laugh and talk about the Philly trip and the Bulls the rest of the way to school.

. . .

I see Grace in the hallway a few periods into the school day. I get to tell her about spring break in Philly. She tells me that she worked all week. I admit that I missed her a lot.

"I missed you too, Molotti. Now where is my poem?"

"Not now . . . in time." I smile. "Are we walking to the bus stop after school?" She nods, so I tell her I will see her later. As she walks off, I look at her and think to myself that she had to be perfectly designed by God himself. I want to ask her about Derrick but decide to wait and see if she brings it up.

I walk down to lunch and see they've moved everyone to the school auditorium. I ask security what's going on and he tells me that the lines in the hallway to get into lunch are too crazy.

"Just go in, take a seat, and we will call you in row by row."

The girls are all sitting on one side of the auditorium and the guys on the other. I assume the lines got too crazy because the lunchroom just recently began serving nachos with melted cheese, ground beef, and jalapeño peppers, and they're super popular. Whenever the bell rings, people race downstairs to get them because they don't have enough for everybody. I also figure that the lines get so cluttered that it starts fights. I guess this is a shrewd move by security.

I'm sitting eight rows up when Alvin and some of the guys from the S.O.A. gang stroll in. They all walk to the front and start laughing and joking around. Then Tony, one of the leaders that everyone calls White Boy because of his light skin and wavy hair, walks toward Elliot in the front row. White Boy grabs Elliot by the shirt, snatches him off the seat, and says, "Dude, get to the back and then sit down."

Elliot doesn't say a word, just puts his head down and walks to the back. Alvin and a few of the other guys push a couple more guys out of their seats and sit down, laughing. People are furious, but say nothing. After a short while, they call everyone into the lunchroom. Those in back never get nachos. I sit in the lunchroom with Preston, as always, and he tells me he thinks Alvin will always be a part of them. I say, "Yeah, maybe."

After school, while I'm waiting on Grace, the football coach walks up to me.

"Hey, young fella, I would love for you to come to our summer camp and play football."

I look at him, shocked. "Really?"

"Yeah, man. I been seeing you working out in the gym; we can use someone with your work ethic and determination."

"Determination I have to work on, but I'm on the rowing team," I tell him. He looks at me as if I'm cracking a joke.

"Listen, man, that's not a real sport, and it's not going to take you anywhere," he tells me with a finger to the chest. "Football is the heart and soul of public schools and our community. You should be a part of something big. You can row boats for fun and games."

I want to tell him that we're the first all-black public-school row team, that's historic, and that rowing is real and harder than anything I've ever tried, but I choke.

"Okay, I will let you know," I say instead, and he slaps me on the shoulder.

"That's the spirit. I see a leader in you."

I feel a little disrespected, but I'm not going to step up to the football coach—a well-built and intimidating guy.

When Grace comes down, we walk to the bus stop and I talk to her about the football coach and how I feel. I tell her I feel like no one respects the idea of us rowing. I'm very frustrated and feel like none of the teachers respect it either. I think some parents, and a lot of the kids here, only see it as some recreational activity if it's not basketball or football.

"I respect it," Grace tells me.

"That's why you're so damn cool."

She is always supportive, always says the right things. I look at her and wonder how I *couldn't* fall in love with this girl. She is like the month of May in the wintertime. God has blessed her with the spirit of wisdom, knowledge, and understanding. After talking to her, I sprint back to the gym as usual to get ready for row practice, hoping that the coaches are there.

When I get to the gym I see Ken, half the team from the Philly trip, and a few new freshmen. I know some guys won't continue on the team because they have to babysit their little brothers and sisters and others have to work after school to help parents pay the bills.

"Okay, guys, the coaches won't be here today," he says.

"Did they all quit?" I ask.

He chuckles. "They're just taking the day off," he replies. I take a deep breath and nod.

"Okay," Ken says, "since the coaches aren't here, we are going to the field house for swim practice. If you have your shorts and T-shirt I'll meet you down at the bus. If you don't, take the day off."

While we're waiting by the bus, I can hear Ken on the phone yelling at Lupe. He hangs up.

"I guess I'll be driving today."

"Let me guess, she is passed out somewhere," Malcolm says, and we start laughing.

The bus is still in the parking lot from the weekend, and Alvin asks Ken if he has driven a bus before or if he should call his dad.

"I haven't, actually," Ken says. "Can you call him?"

Alvin calls, but his dad is still at work. Ken reassures us, "It will be fine. It's like driving a car." I feel like something is wrong with this situation, but I'm used to seeing crazier things than this so I shrug it off.

We head to the field house and it's a pretty smooth ride. People hanging out on the corners look at us like we're crazy. It is pretty unusual to see a big white school bus with $7,000 on the window and the hood roll by. When we get to the Fillmore swimming pool, there are lifeguards there ready to work on our swimming. It goes pretty smoothly and we learn some new techniques. It seems like the only time the team is calm now is when we're in the water. I'm not sure if it's because the water makes us feel a sense of peace . . . or fear. I just know it works.

When we're done swimming, we get back on the Marshmallow Man. While driving down Roosevelt Road, Malcolm starts goofing off and horsing around with the freshmen in the back of the bus. Ken yells to cut it out. When one freshman gets a little rough, Malcolm grabs a bottle of baby powder left on the bus from Philly, and pours it all over him. A baby powder cloud quickly fills up the bus, so Ken pulls into a gas station on the corner of Independence Boulevard and Roosevelt Road. I hear people on the corner making jokes.

"Damn, those li'l niggas have the bus smoked out!"

"What y'all smoking?"

Ken stops the bus and yells for Malcolm and the freshmen to cut it out before he kicks them off the team. The guys in the back take seats and chill out. Meanwhile, the whole gas station is staring at the bus. People are shaking their heads, pointing, and whispering to one another. Ken pulls out and heads back toward the school.

Preston says, "This is ghetto."

"Yeah, you know you ghetto when you confuse baby powder for weed smoking," Elliot tells him. Malcolm jumps in.

"You know you ghetto when you have a hanger on your TV as an antenna, Elliot." Everyone starts laughing.

"You know you ghetto if you still have a TV that you have to put on U to get to the double digits," I say. Everyone starts getting in on the joke.

"You know you ghetto when you put baby powder on your neck."

"You know you ghetto when you stick batteries in the freezer."

"You know you ghetto when your mom fills the bathtub with clothes and water, and has the kids stomp on it and pretend to be a real machine," I say.

"To come up with that one, you must really do that," Malcolm says, and everyone laughs. We keep playing ghetto jokes all the way back to the school.

When we pull up to the school the block is filled with people hanging out, girls jumping rope, boys dribbling basketballs, old men drinking beer, old ladies talking, and guys playing dice. Ken makes a left into the parking lot and we hear a crazy crunching sound as the bus lurches up and sideways. I look out the window to my left and see the bus on top of a red car. I know that this can't be good.

We see a woman and about ten dudes running toward the bus. They are screaming, yelling, and cursing, and we're all terrified. The whole block runs over. Ken seems to be keeping his cool, but I can tell he's scared. The lady is yelling up at Ken, "That's my car. Get the hell off this bus."

A guy holding up his fist says, "Come take this beating."

Ken tells us to calm down, and I say, "Let's get off and talk."

Everyone else says, "Don't open that bus door. You're crazy."

I shake my head. "I thought you guys are big-time gang members that aren't scared of anything. You're gonna let this man go by himself?"

Alvin says, "Let's go."

Ken, Alvin, and I walk off the bus while everyone else stays on. The lady gets in Ken's face and says, "That's my ride."

Ken pulls out a checkbook and says, "Get a pen."

All the guys on the sidewalk watching shut their mouths as if they've never seen a checkbook before. The lady asks someone to get her a pen. Ken writes something in his checkbook and hands her the check. "No cops necessary."

She looks at the check, throws both her arms in the air as if she's about to fly, and smiles at him.

"Hey, homie, you cool with me."

"Cool."

The whole block sits and waits for Ken to move the bus, and I realize that money can get you out of almost anything.

He dislodges our bus and it's destroyed. We ask him how much the check was written for, but he tells us not to worry about it. I am so curious to know. Alvin looks over at Malcolm, who stayed on the bus.

"What happened to you, big guy? Why weren't you out there with us?"

"I have nothing to do with that."

Ken tells us that this event stays between us, and we agree and depart the bus.

Alvin invites me over to his place to watch the Bulls game. I'm intrigued by his loyalty and know that he's the kind of friend I want. When we get to his place we take a seat on his porch. His neighbor walks out of his apartment next door and stares us both down; Alvin acts as if nothing's happening.

"Why that dude look at us like that?" I ask him.

"It's all good. He still mad because we flipped his car over on New Year's Eve."

"What?" I ask, surprised.

"Yeah, we were bored. But we flipped it back."

"How many guys?"

"Like, five," Alvin says. "He'll get over it."

I see Alvin's dad, Big Al, pull up and it's suddenly like the world has changed. People who were standing in front of Big Al's house walk away. The drug addicts and dealers all wave and speak to him. All the kids pick up the trash from his yard. It's like the whole block fears him. Even Alvin changes; he seems timid.

"Hey, Dad."

"Where are your sisters and brothers?"

"Upstairs."

"That's good. And the house is clean, right?"

Alvin tells him he thinks so, and Big Al says, "Well, go on and get up there."

I say hello to him and he says, "What's up." We walk upstairs into the house together, straight into the kitchen, where I say hello to Alvin's sister Angie. She says hello back without looking at me. I also meet his younger sister Diana. They all clean while I sit there, and Big Al tells jokes that aren't funny but we laugh anyway. I think we are just laughing out of fear. Big Al takes the chain off the refrigerator and puts it in his room.

I get up and open the refrigerator to see what's inside and Alvin says, "Boy, what you doing?" and slams it closed. His sisters look at me like I'm crazy.

I sit back down, and end up playing spades with Alvin, his dad, and his brothers for the next couple of hours. The Temptations are playing on the radio the whole time; Big Al schools me on the oldies. I tell Alvin it's getting late and I want to go home and catch the Bulls game before it starts. He asks his dad if he can walk me to the train.

Big Al says, "Who in the hell is going to walk you back?" Alvin just looks shocked. But his dad says he's kidding, but to come right back.

We head downstairs and there are a few guys from Alvin's block chilling on the porch, talking about their money-making scheme. Alvin asks what they got going on and they ask him if he wants to make some money.

"Doing what?"

"Well, you know the Bulls are hot right now," this guy Tone says, "and there's a game at the United Center. What we been doing is driving the car to the game when it's over. I stand out there and see which white folks are drunk. You know they be up in the stadium getting messed up. If they pull out keys, that means they got a car. So we follow them to the car, and if they're driving, my boy will pull up with his car and drive in front of them. When they drive out into the street, he slams on the brakes.

"The guy hits us, and we jump out of the car and yell at them, 'Are you drunk?' When they get scared, we tell them to give us three hundred dollars or we calling the police. Sometimes we have to go to the cash machine, but it's worth it. We make over a thousand each time."

Alvin says, "Damn."

I tell them it's really creative. "You never get caught?"

Tone looks at me, then at Alvin. "Who this?"

"He's cool."

Tone says they need another driver to make more money and Alvin backs off. "Next time though, dog."

We both walk to the train talking about how creative they are, and about life and family. I ask Alvin why his dad talks so bad about his mom. He says it's because she doesn't support them. "But I want to kill him every time he does. Don't get me wrong, I love my dad. I just don't like when he talks about my mom."

"Tell me about your mom, bruh," I say.

"Man, it's nothing you need to know about my mom."

"Gotch, but if she ever needs someone to talk to, she can hang with my mom. She is a very spiritual woman."

"Cool," he says quietly.

"How often you see her?"

"Every other day, man. My mom and dad just don't speak."

We arrive at the Blue Line and I thank him for having me over. I tell him I'll be at his place in the morning to wake him up for school.

"Dude, you don't have to do that, I'll be up."

"Cool," I tell him and get on the train.

On the way home I think about Ken driving the bus and how crazy Alvin and I are for stepping off with him. I also think about Alvin's family, and what I noticed just by being at his house for a few hours. His dad is an ex-cop with a quick temper. He has many guns hidden around the house and doesn't trust anyone. He hires drug addicts in the neighborhood to clean the yards and to fix things around the house. Big Al preaches family and says there's nothing above that. He's very old-fashioned and is the only provider in the house, so he feels like there is only one voice. What Big Al says, goes—no questions asked.

I can tell that Alvin is his favorite and that they're the closest. He says that Alvin's siblings' problems will probably land him in jail or kill him. He told me Alvin's problem is that he is too damn loyal. Alvin didn't say a word as his dad spoke. Their family bonds every day over spades. I've never seen an immediate family so close. I think Alvin's sisters are gorgeous, and I sense that no one in the neighborhood thinks twice about crushing on them. Big Al and Alvin's brothers are fighters, and they would die to protect each other.

The next morning, I arrive at Alvin's place at 7 a.m. and ring the doorbell. Angie comes to open the door and I walk up behind her, trying hard to not stare at her backside. I get to the kitchen and see a chain on the refrigerator still. When I get to Alvin's room, he is knocked out sleeping.

"Alvin, it's time to get up."

Pooh Trigga starts to stir. "Damn, dude. Don't be coming here early all in our face."

Alvin pleads, "Go to school, I will be there for second period."

"Come on, man, get up. I'll wait for you."

"I'm saying, though," Pooh Trigga says, "you come here with the 'woo wat the bang,' that's not cool, but it is what it is."

Alvin says, "Yeah, I know."

I'm lost in the conversation and realize that since my mom got out of the home I haven't been hanging with the guys from the hood. I've lost my ability to interpret slang. I'm pretty sure he's trying to say that since I'm already here, Alvin should just get up and go with me.

Alvin finally rises to get dressed. I wait in the kitchen, trying my best to spark a conversation with Angie, but to no avail. It's almost as if she was told not to interact with her brother's guy friends. Alvin walks in, and yells, "Boy, don't get flatlined talking to my sister, now let's go." I respond with "amen."

On my way to lunch later, I'm walking down the hallway and get shoulder shoved by a kid named Melvin. I'm not sure if it's on purpose or an accident, but I tell him to watch it. He turns around with his fist balled up, walks toward me and says, "Or what?" People around us stop what they're doing and stare at us. I look him in the eyes and one part of my brain is telling me to hit him and man up, while the other part of my brain is thinking about my future.

I just say, "After school."

"Cool. I will meet you after school." We both walk away.

I've never been suspended from school in my life, and I wonder what the hell just happened. If I fight this dude, I'll be suspended for sure. I think about what I told Alvin on the bus in Philly about being the bigger person and I know I have to practice what I preach. The problem is this dude wants to fight. I just try to clear my mind and wait for the time to come. I think about trying to clear it up, but I live in a place where doing that means people will consider me a punk. I would accept that to avoid getting suspended, but I think about Grace. I know every girl in our school loves a man who can fight, but I also know that Grace isn't that kind of girl. I think about what other people will say to her or what she will hear.

When I get to the auditorium for lunch the front two rows are empty. The third row to the back is completely full. I guess the guys are too scared to sit there because the S.O.A. gang will embarrass them or beat them up. I decide to walk to the front and sit there. Elliot and some of the guys from the crew team look at me like I've lost my mind.

A minute later, some of the S.O.A. guys come in and walk straight to the front. Everyone is looking. Alvin sits down next to me, and White Boy walks up.

"Hey, man, I saw you on the block yesterday. Al's boy, right?"

I nod yes, and he shakes my hand and sits down next to me. I swallow my spit and finally take a breath. I guess if I'm cool with Alvin, I'm cool with them.

When the last bell rings, I head downstairs to meet Grace so I can walk her to the bus stop. I see Melvin at the bottom of the stairs and my heart drops, because I know I'm about to have an actual fistfight. As I'm taking off my bookbag, Melvin walks up to me and apologizes.

"Sorry about earlier. It wasn't cool, it won't happen again." He reaches out to shake my hand. I shake his hand and tell him it's all good, trying to look as though I expected an apology all along.

He walks away and I stand there trying to figure out what just happened. I wonder if he saw me sitting in the front of the auditorium with Alvin and decided to make peace. I'm relieved because I don't want to fight Melvin. He looks like he's having a bad day just like I was when my mom told me about my grandfather. I guess every day is a bad day when you live where we live.

8

Race Day

Running up the school stairs comes easy for me these days. Being in shape makes you feel alive and mentally well-balanced. As I walk toward the gym door, I walk past the football team stretching in the hallway. They always have something dumb to say. One of the guys shouts out, "How is rowing those slave ships?" Everyone starts laughing. "Ha ha," I reply, and walk into the gym. It's quiet, and the team is seated at center court. I toss my backpack to the side and run to get seated. Coach Jessica has the floor. Just about half of the team from Philly is present. I figured after the trip that some people wouldn't come back. For most, because they had just wanted to go out of town and for others, they have gotten a taste of how demanding this sport really is. In the circle is Arthur, Elliot, Malcolm, Preston, Ronald, Pheodus, Leah, Leslie, Alvin, and Pooh Trigga. Just enough folks for a boy's eight boat but not enough girls for a boat. The tragic thing about the sport is that if one person doesn't show to get on the water, we don't go out. Rowing is the ultimate team sport.

. . .

Coach Jessica has this deadpan look on her face as she begins talking.

"You guys have joined the team, practiced through winter training, and just got back from spring break camp. Give yourself a hand." Everyone claps. "Now, what we are looking for is that you guys stay committed so we can race at the Chicago Sprints this summer. It's one of the biggest Midwest races, and it's at the Lincoln Park Lagoon."

Malcolm raises his hand. "If it's about spandex uniforms, put your hand down, Malcolm," Coach Jessica says. He puts his hand down. "We want to enter a boy's eight for 1,000 meters." There is a mixture of excitement and uneasiness in the room. "What about the girls?" Leslie shouts. "If you can get the girls to come to practice, we can row a four," Coach Jessica says. "I want to row with the boys," Leah adds. "Oh, hell naw," Malcolm and Preston say at the same time.

"Who will we race?" I ask.

Coach Jessica says, "Let me finish, please, then ask questions at the end.

"You guys will race the local private schools. Not sure who yet. So, training will be every day after school at the lagoon, and on days that it rains, we will practice indoors on the erg. We will be working on rowing techniques and drilling the shit out of you all. We have a couple of months. This will be the first time an all-black team rows at the Sprints. Let's get it together. Now, other good news." Everyone starts laughing and cheering.

"The *Chicago Tribune* will come to visit next week to interview some of you guys and watch you row at a practice." The gymnasium goes berserk. "Okay, listen up," Coach Jessica demands. "It will be next Thursday and please wear shorts and a T-shirt and be prepared to work hard that day. Now get the ergs, and let's get ready for practice." Preston jumps up, singing "Mo Money Mo Problems" by Biggie. Then everyone else joins in. We quickly pull out the erg machines and everyone is pumped. While we're training, some of the guys from the football team come in and make a beat on the wall and start beatboxing "Row, Row, Row Your

Boat." They start laughing and making fun of us. One of the captains, a stocky bald dude named Colby, says, "Have fun rowing, guys."

"I can do what you do anytime of the day," I tell him, "but I bet you can't last three minutes full force on this machine."

"I wouldn't waste my time. Look downstairs in the trophy case at the North Lawndale paper, buddy . . . we exist."

They walk out singing again and Malcolm starts laughing. I tell him he has no loyalty.

"Man, chill out, they're playing."

I keep quiet and go back to training. I'm not happy at all. I take this rowing team seriously. I feel like the football coach sent them in here to do that because he knows I don't want to join. After practice, I ask Alvin if he thinks the same thing and he tells me I'm overthinking it. I tell him he's probably right and head home.

When I get home, my mom seems very sad.

"What's wrong, Mom?" I ask.

"I am having problems with your little brother. He's starting to act like his father, and by the way, Ike went into the home."

"They let him in? Even though he stole all those coats?"

"Yes. Forgiveness is a big part of our faith," she tells me, tearing up. "I still don't know why you're so good, and your brothers are so rebellious. What happened when I was away in the home?"

I tell her we pretty much did what we wanted. I want to say to her that her bad decisions have a ripple effect on us, but I know she already knows that. She's been working hard to fix that. It doesn't make sense to make her feel bad, because she had a rough childhood as well.

"Mom, I learned how to be a good kid from a teacher and watching *The Fresh Prince of Bel-Air*, *Family Matters*, and *A Different World*. While my brothers stayed out late, I stayed home and watched TV. I learned how to talk to my elders, what to avoid, and how to be a good friend. I was so jealous of those characters because I wanted what they had, but I loved them at the same time." I explain to her that it was like Uncle

Phil became my dad, Dwayne Wayne was my brother, and Steve Urkel was my friend. "They made me laugh, and I learned from their mistakes. These shows held me together during my greatest depression. I know for a fact that I am stronger because of them. I know that doesn't happen to everyone, but I wanted it. I just really wanted it."

She looks at me, amazed.

"You know what, Arshay? Many are called, but few are chosen. I believe you are chosen."

"Thanks, Mom. I will talk to Issac."

"Okay, son," she replies.

I walk into my room, and Isaac is playing his handheld video game.

"Hey, bruh, let me holla at you," I say.

"What you want?" he replies with no eye contact.

"Why are you giving Mom a hard time?"

"Too much God stuff, bruh, I'm not with it."

"Well that God stuff changed our family life, so get with it."

"She never does anything for me. My grandmother is the one who took care of me," he says in a huff.

"Not right; our mom is doing her best for us now."

"Man, you come and go as you please, and I can't go nowhere, that's straight favoritism."

"Dude, every time you go out you get into a fight or cause a problem," I tell him. "If you want to do what you want, do what I do. Come home and do the dishes without being asked. Pray in the morning, stop falling asleep at church, stop getting in trouble in school, and start doing things with Mom and see how things change. Until then, stop complaining."

He just says I'm lame and looks at me like I'm dumb. It seems like the more I try to become a better person for myself and others, the more shit I get. I don't care, though, because I'm on a mission: to love my team more, love my family more, and love myself more. I will work hard to not lose my brother at home, because if we do, we'll lose him to the streets like we lost Shaundell, who is out there banging.

All week at school, I have nothing but practice, Chicago Sprints, and the *Chicago Tribune* on my mind. Afterschool consists of a forty-five-minute ride to the boathouse, getting dressed, pulling out the oars, stretching, a one-mile run around the Lagoon, taking out the boat, and drilling for an hour and a half. The drills require perfection. Eight crew members coming together as one to drop the blade in the water at the catch, drive, finish, and recover all at the same time, repeatedly. Coach Jessica has been coxing us, and I can't get her voice out of my head. "Arms only, arms and body, half slide, full slide, quarter feather, full feather, and let it run," over and over again. That's what we hear all day, every day. We call it the pick drill. The practice is better when there is no wind, the water is flat, and you can hear the sound of your oarlocks working. Some rowers say that after the countless strokes you feel supernatural. I haven't felt that yet. For me, it has been a lot of splashing water, blisters, and lower back pains. One thing that has my attention is that the same eight guys and two girls keep showing up. Today they earned a chance to be in the *Tribune* shot, and I am stoked.

When we arrive at the Lincoln Park boathouse to row, the camera crew is already working with Eugene. Eugene is a slightly overweight African American man perpetually clad in an orange hoodie. He's the caretaker for the Lincoln Park boathouse, and he stands out like a sore thumb as the only black person around besides us. We never speak to him; we actually kind of make fun of him behind his back. He never says a word, but he always watches us practice and I can tell he's proud. I look out into the water and see the St. Ignatius and Loyola Academy crew teams practicing. We share the water with them and a couple of other high school teams. These are primarily all-white private schools that have long histories of successful crew teams. They have dedicated coaches, well-funded teams, and athletes that are far from just having learned to swim. They represent the other side of the river from Manley. The side we're rowing to get across to. And we will.

I am a little nervous about which of them we will face at the Chicago Sprints because every time I see them practice they have perfect timing, flawless execution, and every stroke seems to send a shock of electricity through the water. But today the *Chicago Tribune* is here to see us, the Manley Crew Team. Coach Jessica tells us to get dressed so we can start. We stare back at her, and tell her we didn't bring our workout clothes.

"Are you kidding me?" she asks.

Everyone eyes Coach Jessica, who looks like she feels awful. I can't speak for everyone, but today I dressed up pretty fly because I know we will be on the front page of the sports paper. I have some freshly creased blue jeans on, a new flannel shirt, and a fresh haircut. This is not the right protocol for practice, but when you are from where I am from, sometimes you only get one shot to shine. So, I will be in the paper looking good for Grace to see. Coach Jessica looks at us, disappointed, and tells us to get to work. Some of us who are not attired for practice will be uncomfortable but will deal.

The *Tribune* interviews Ken, Preston, and Arthur. I'm hurt because I'm not chosen to do an interview. I feel like I'm the mature and loyal one on the team, but Arthur is the team captain and Preston has a lot of personality. Preston is the coaches' favorite, and I don't stand out or have crazy talent, so I'm always on the back burner. I'm the guy who has to work really hard to get noticed, and I'm pretty sure it will always be that way for me. I'm used to it, so I just keep my feelings to myself.

The *Tribune* crew follows us as we start our workout. All eyes from other high school crews are on us. Some folks from St. Ignatius are laughing, and I think it's because we didn't properly dress. But again, no one is interviewing them. We walk the boat to the dock and it's a bit of a struggle to get in. The jeans are hindering my flexibility. I think to myself, *Never again am I wearing these clothes to row.* I notice a crew member from the *Tribune* cracking a smirk at us as well. We had a sweet push off from the dock with Leah in the stroke seat; Malcolm is in seven, Preston is in six, Ronald is in five, Arthur's in four, Elliot's in three, I am in two, and Alvin is in the bow. The weather is like a perfect 75 degrees; the water is like glass, and the cameras are flashing. Because we did not correctly dress, we only go down the course a couple of times for the photographer. After practice, while the camera crew is packing everything away, Alvin comes out of the locker room upset, saying he's "about to kick this white boy ass." We ask what happened and he says that one of the rowers from the other team said to his buddy that we don't deserve to be on camera. I get upset instantly and say, "We will get them at the Chicago Sprints, on the water." Coach Victor doesn't know what's going on, but tells us not to embarrass him in front of the cameras. I think maybe he figures we're fighting with each other. I try to open my mouth to tell him what happened, but Coach Victor says to stop or we're done. He tells us to go to the car, so we do.

I walk into school a few days after the practice at the lagoon and a security guard walks over and shakes my hand like I just won the presidency.

"What's up?" I say, confused.

He pulls out the paper and there it is, the whole team is rowing on the front page of the *Chicago Tribune* Sports section.

"Congratulations, young man," he says.

"Can I have that?" I ask.

"Sure, I have a few of them. You guys are making us Wildcats proud." All the teachers and the principal are excited for us. Some of the guys from the rowing team are by the main office, and they are all being praised. There is vibrant energy throughout the school, as if one of our teams just won a championship. I notice that when the teachers and staff are excited, the mood of the whole school changes. It's rare to see all the teachers so happy all at once.

Colby and a couple guys from the football team walk past, and it's a perfect opportunity for a comeback. I yell out, "Where's that North Lawndale paper of yours?"

"It's in the trophy case, where it belongs." I can tell he doesn't know what's going on, so I hand him the *Tribune* with us on the front page.

"Can you put this next to it? We exist."

He looks at it, throws it back at me, and says, "Good job, niggas." We start laughing and he goes over to shake Alvin's hand. Alvin and Colby are from the same block and have respect for each other.

When I get to class they announce that we're in the paper. A woman reads the article from the *Chicago Tribune* over the intercom so we can all hear. I pick up my paper and read along. The headline reads, MAN-LEY'S CREW PROGRAM SHATTERS STEREOTYPES ABOUT BLACK ATHLETES, BUT MORE IMPORTANT, IT HAS A POSITIVE ACADEMIC IMPACT.

The woman finishes reading the article over the intercom and everyone starts clapping. I feel like we're finally on our way. It's the first time I've been a part of something huge and I think about what Ken told us on the first day of practice: if we work hard, we will succeed. I can't wait to get home and paste the paper on my wall. The quote that stuck out to me is "That's right, there's a crew team on the West Side, where you're supposed to dunk basketballs, not coxswains." I was so excited I couldn't stop shaking. My other favorite quote is by Ken: "I would love to have a fast boat, but I am more interested in using rowing to keep kids in school, increase their self-esteem, and help us get admitted to colleges with good financial aid packages." I am pumped to get back on the water.

After school, Ken and Coach Jessica are waiting for us in the back. Ken tells us that there's no more Lupe and we'll be traveling to practice in his Jeep and Coach Jessica's car. They tell us who has made the final cut for the Chicago Sprints: Arthur, Malcolm, Preston, Alvin, Pheodus, Elliot, Ronald, and myself with Pooh Trigga as a spare. Everyone else has quit or wasn't taking the team seriously and for us, our reason to continue is bigger than our reason to quit.

Summer of '98 is here and, for the last couple of months, training has been both incredible and trying. We row on misty days, extremely sunny days, and when the water is choppy. We are learning to weather the storm on all occasions. Dealing with exhaustion and pain has become a part of my life in this sport. If you can hang in there and not let discouragement take over, you may just learn something about yourself. This summer, I have become the hardest worker I know. The guys on the team are not perfect, but every day is like the potter's house. Rowing is chipping away the negative and adding what needs to be there. We learn to sit tall, relax, and breathe in our sessions. Most practice days, we are missing Pooh Trigga, Arthur, or Ronald because they are doing senior-year graduation stuff. So, at times we end up rowing in a four-boat and rotating between positions. We feel strong and can move the boat well, but our timing and balance are usually off, and we spend a lot of time working on it. Of course, there is still so much goofing off on the boat that Coach Jessica will stand up in the coxswain seat and let us have it. I also notice that she is starting to feel uncomfortable with all the flirting Preston is doing with her.

It's our last day of practice before the Chicago Sprints, and there are four teams in our category for the novice four. We will not race the eight because there are never eight guys here to practice, usually a six or seven as of late. Who will be the four? I am not sure. It's between Malcolm, Preston, Alvin, Arthur, Pheodus, Elliot, and myself. Malcolm is the Hercules of the team, but he always stops when he is tired, and you can't do that in rowing. Preston has the most beautiful stroke, but he just doesn't have enough power right now. Elliot is too short. So I am going to go with the most consistently strong guys with excellent cardio: me, Alvin, Arthur, and Phedous for the four, but I can be wrong. I am ready to haul ass and prove that this is not some pilot program. This is our last row down the course.

"Okay, guys, we are going to row the whole 1,000 meters. For the first 200, we are going to row 34 strokes per minute and settle in at a 28 until 200 to go, then you give all you got," Coach Jessica says from the coxswain's seat. In the boat now are me, Arthur, Alvin, and Elliot. Malcolm, Preston, and Pheodus just got out of the boat. "Okay, blades buried. Ready, set, row!"

We take off. I'm in the two-seat rowing port, and I can feel the spray of the stroke-seat blade splashing water back at me. "Balance the boat!" I yell. We find our timing and hit 200 meters. We settle in, driving hard and recovering. Driving and recovering. We reach 600 meters, and I feel the boat slow. My pulse quickens. "We're halfway there! Keep pushing! You have been through much harder than this!" Coach screams. I kick up the gears even though my body is ready to give in. But when you no longer can row with your legs, you must row with your heart. Now 200 to go. "Lighten fast," Coach calls. My mind starts playing tricks on me, saying shit like *you're not built for balancing boats, callused hands, open water, and regattas*—that I don't belong in this ancient sport so long reserved for schools like Harvard and Yale, Oxford and Cambridge. Places light-years away from the West Side of Chicago. In this moment, I am in a game of tug-of-war between the me in the boat and the me the world expects. But I am not the only one fighting here. My muscles surge with adrenaline as my team pushes forward in unison.

After we put the boat away, we get tired waiting for Coach Jessica. Being on the water is the only thing that calms the storm in us. Coach Jessica opens by saying, "This is your first and last race of the season. We will continue to work out this summer and open the school year with two fall races in St. Louis and Iowa."

"That's what's up," Preston says. Coach Jessica goes on to explain that "the Chicago Sprints will have a ton of people and most of them don't look like you. When you get on the water, you row about 600 meters down the course to the start line. When the flag drops, you go with the practice plan. Keep your head in the boat and don't stop. Those are the rules. And if you catch a crab, you recover it and keep going."

. . .

I'm terrified of catching a crab. A crab happens when a rower can't remove the oar blade from the water at the finish of the drive (the part of the stroke where the rower is pulling), and a sloppy stroke occurs. This can happen when a rower loses his grip on the handle, makes an error in judging when to remove or release the blade from the water, or if the boat tips to the side and there's nowhere for the rower to lower their hands to remove the blade. This usually means some timing problems for a few strokes. An over-the-head crab is even more serious. It's when the oar handle forces the rower onto his back and the handle goes over his head. This usually means the crew has to stop rowing, recover the oar, and then continue. I've even heard of people being choked by an oar, or having the oar handle get caught in a rower's stomach. The rower gets thrown out of the boat and the rest of the crew has to stop to get the rower back into the boat.

"Okay, guys, let's bring it in," Coach Victor says proudly. We say, "One, two, three, Manley Crew," then we break. Usually after practices Coach Jessica, Coach Victor, and Ken drive us all home, dropping us off one by one. They all are far too kind, and I know their belief in us is limitless.

Race day turns out to be a sunny morning in Chicago. We meet at the school, with Ken and Coach Jessica arriving after most of us. But Alvin and Pooh Trigga are nowhere to be found until a loud, smoking car zips into the school parking lot. We are relieved they've made it, though Ken is curious about the car. I tell him it belongs to Pooh, and that the neighborhood calls it the "Illegal Pooh Trigga Regal." It's a gray Regal with stolen plates and a muffler attached by a wire hanger.

Pooh Trigga tells Ken he can't make it because he has to work. "But one question," Pooh shouts after Ken. "How much was that check that you wrote that lady when the bus was on top of her car?"

We laugh and Ken shakes his head.

We're quiet on the way to the lagoon because we're so full of nerves. Even though practice has been going well, we're all still uneasy because we will be the only black people out there. When we arrive there are hundreds of people spread out in tents, and almost none of them have brown faces. We've invited our parents, teachers, staff, and some students but no one is here, and I'm not really surprised. I had a feeling no one would show up for us. I guess that's what Colby meant when he said, "We exist." The football and basketball games are always packed.

Around us, families are chilling on the grass, eating bagels, playing catch, and setting up seats to watch the race. There are camera crews everywhere and I can't count the number of knots I feel in my stomach. Every rower I see looks flawless. They all look tall, handsome, lean, reserved, and are all wearing team Speedos, of course. Our team decided earlier that we'd all quit before we wear a Speedo; Malcolm said that you can't pay a black man to wear a Speedo, and if you can, they aren't black anymore. Our uniform consists of basketball shorts, cut-off-sleeve T-shirts, and headbands.

I can feel eyes burning holes through my skin, and I whisper to Preston to see if he notices, too.

"Yeah, they looking at us like we're contagious."

Alvin is walking around checking out the white girls, giving them winks, and trying to talk to a few of them. They just seem scared and walk off as we laugh. I split off for a walk by myself while everyone else goes to check out girls. I can see that Arthur and Elliot are making themselves at home talking to some girls in the Kenwood Academy tent.

I stare at the city skyline on my walk, lost in thought. I look at the Lincoln Park Lagoon and the Lincoln Park Zoo on the West Side. To the east of the lagoon is Lake Shore Drive, a busy expressway, and then Lake Michigan. Sometimes during rush hour, while we're rowing in the lagoon, I see people staring at us in disbelief or honking their horns. On my walk back I see a crowd around Malcolm and hear someone laughing. There's a journalist holding up a recorder while Malcolm spouts off.

"It's like Tiger Woods going into golf. It's like Venus and Serena going into tennis. It's like Jackie Robinson going into baseball or Jack Johnson going into boxing. We will dominate!"

I shake my head and walk away.

Later, Ken brings us in and explains that Mike O'Gorman, the coach who taught us in Philly, will push us off and that after our race there will be an erg competition. They will pick two guys from each team to race each other 500 meters and 1,000 meters on the machine. The coaches must have just decided this today, because this is the first I hear of this. Or maybe it's just to give the members of the team who won't make the lineup a chance to compete. In the circle is Alvin, Preston, Arthur, Pheodus, Elliot, Malcom, and myself. Mike announces that the rowers for this race are Malcolm in four seat, Arthur in three seat, myself in two, and Pheodus in bow. Coach Jessica will be the coxswain, which means she'll help steer the boat and give us encouragement and direction during the race. Alvin and Preston aren't happy they aren't rowing, but Coach Jessica tells them they will row in St. Louis in the fall. "This is bullshit!" Alvin shouts, walking away.

"How this dude calling shots and he hasn't even been here to coach us?" Malcolm whispers to me.

I shrug, telling him to shut up. Mike tells us that there are many different teams here: University of Chicago, Northwestern, different boathouses, and other high school teams. He tells us to go meet some new friends. We all think the same thing: *Yeah, right.* "Just kidding!" he says, cracking himself up.

"This dude and his Seinfeld jokes," Malcolm whispers. "Not funny."

Mike explains to us that the lagoon is a 1,000 meter sprint race against our opponent, St. Ignatius. I look around for the other team but don't see them anywhere. I can hear excitement in his voice as he tells us to take ten minutes to chill out before we come back to pre-race stretching with Coach Victor.

After stretching with Coach Victor we head to the slings to get our shell and start the long walk to the dock. As we get to the dock, Eugene, the boathouse caregiver, is the dockmaster, the person who controls the dock traffic. It feels good to see another black person around. We have never been this quiet. We dip the boat into the water and Pheodus doubles back into the boathouse. None of us knows what he's doing until we see him come running back out with a life jacket on. People are giggling and we all redden with embarrassment.

"Nigga, what you doing?" Malcolm whispers to him.

"I'm not going to drown."

None of us looks up because we don't want to see the reaction from the crowd. Malcolm implores him to take the life jacket off through gritted teeth, but Coach Jessica tells us to cool down and not to make a scene.

We get into the boat and slowly push off the dock and Coach Jessica coxes us to the starting line. People stop eating their sandwiches and walk over to see us. I keep repeating to myself, "*It's our time*." It is something they always say in church. I look out into the crowd one more time and see that out of all the teachers, friends, and parents we invited, only one person actually showed up. It's the special education teacher. He's a white guy, so he blends in with the crowd. I imagine that people are whispering to each other that no one came to support us.

"*Ready!*"

The official holds up a red flag. And it's time to race!

We head up to the catch and I see the St. Ignatius team to our right, looking confident in matching maroon and white outfits, gelled hair, and perfect bone structure. One of their rowers looks back at me with a smirk, and I feel like the world is spinning. My core is shaking, my legs feel weak, and the hair is standing up on the back of my neck. I can sure use a time-out.

The man drops the flag and yells "*Go!*" and we start rowing with all our power, side by side.

Almost immediately, I can feel our boat turning to the left, the opposite way of the other team. We begin rowing harder, and I can see Coach screaming something but can't understand. I also see the crowd screaming. I look behind me, and—*BANG*—our boat slams into the brick wall of the lagoon. I can hear people saying things around me and making lots of noise. We quickly push off with our oars and I look back and see that the St. Ignatius team is about three boat lengths in front of us. We quickly start rowing again, and—*bang*—we crash again. People are covering their mouths, trying not to scream or laugh. We stop rowing and Pheodus starts smacking his oar against the brick. Malcolm yells out that he and I are too strong to row on the same side and he thinks Mike set us up. Coach Jessica yells back at him that he's being ridiculous, and everyone begins arguing with one another. I put my head down, and when I peek up the crowd is staring.

Coach Jessica says, "Okay, let's get out of this. We are going to finish this race."

Malcolm yells back, "No we're not."

"We should go back to the dock," I tell them, but when I look up and see people shaking their heads I change my mind. Now I'm angry. "Let's just finish the race."

"Okay, guys, let's go for it and, Malcolm, less pressure on your end," Coach Jessica demands. We dip our blades in and just go steady-state down the course. St. Ignatius is way ahead of us. Coach Jessica yells for a power ten at the 600-meter mark, and so we pick it up. I can't even look at the crowd I feel so ashamed. The boat is moving, but the timing is off. Chances are everyone is somewhere else mentally. As we come into the last 100 meters St. Ignatius has finished the race and is taking their boat into the dock and looking at us with no expressions. Behind me, Pheodus is crying as we move closer to the finish line. Coach Jessica is trying to calm us down by telling us we did well, but I can feel the negative energy seething. I'm concerned about what Malcolm is going to do or say when we get out of the boat.

We continue to row without a sound and I feel completely spiritless now. We cross the finish line and a few people clap for us, but it doesn't make me feel any better because I know it's out of pity. We turn and work our way back to the dock. At this point, I would pay anything to hear what my teammates are thinking. For the moment, Malcolm is completely silent. But when we pull up to the dock and Ken and Mike grab our oars to pull us in, he yells out again that we were set up to lose.

9

White Tablecloth

"Come on, Malcolm, keep it cool," Ken tells him in a hushed tone, but Malcolm just shakes his head no.

When we get out of the boat, Pheodus takes off running and I storm into the locker room. Malcolm and Arthur stay behind, and Preston and Alvin help take the boat inside. As I sit on the bench in the locker room, a man comes in and puts his hand on my shoulder.

"Who told you it would be easy?"

I look up and see Eugene, the dockmaster.

"No one said it would be easy, but we clearly don't belong in this sport," I say.

"What's your name?"

"Arshay," I tell him. He sits down next to me.

"Arshay, let me tell you a quick story you may have heard before."

"Okay," I say, looking like a sad puppy.

"A man took his young son out to play baseball and told him to throw the ball up to himself and try to swing and hit it for practice. So the kid must have pitched the ball to himself ten times and never could hit the ball. Sad, huh?"

"Yep," I reply, following along.

"So, the father noticed that he kept striking out and felt awful right away. He walked over to his son and said, 'Sorry you couldn't hit the ball, son,' and the little boy looked at his dad with excitement and said, 'Why? This means I'm a great pitcher.'"

I laugh at Eugene's story. "Told him, huh?"

"See, there is a positive side to everything, Arshay. You have to refuse to look at the negative. So what you guys didn't win your first race, or you hit a wall. I tell you this: in ten years, no one will remember that St. Ignatius team, but people are going to remember who you guys are."

"Yeah, but that's because we ran into a brick wall."

"You seem very smart; try to get what I am saying."

I know what Eugene is saying, but I'm being stubborn.

"In no suburb, no inner city, I mean, nowhere in America have I heard of a black public-school team like Manley in a boat to race on a crew team. You guys are the very first! Now that is history. Arshay, my friend, *that* is bigger than winning." He stands up. "So in this race and all the ones to come, people will remember your faces."

I tell Eugene he's a godsend, and he tells me to get back out there with my team because they need me.

"Thanks, man. We have erg races now. Will you watch?"

"With pride."

When I come out of the locker room, people are setting up the erg machines and my team is hanging out in the boathouse. Ken asks if I'm okay, and I tell him I am and I'm ready for the second part. I ask the team if anyone has seen Pheodus.

"Yeah," Preston says, "he's climbing a tree outside the boathouse."

I'm not surprised; Pheodus is a pretty weird guy and doesn't say much. When we were in Philadelphia he barely spoke a word to anyone, so everyone gave him a hard time, including me.

"Malcolm will compete in the 1,000-meter race, and Arshay will compete in the 1,500-meter race," Coach Jessica tells us.

I figure Malcolm is doing the short race because he's super strong but his cardio is poor. I work very hard in practice and have the best cardio.

When we leave the boathouse, people are trying not to look at us. I know that everyone pities us, so I turn on my game face and stretch for the next round.

The first race on the erg is between Malcolm and the guy who rowed stroke seat for St. Ignatius. We gather around Malcolm, hyping him up while the coaches prep his machine. I see Eugene, and he winks at me and nods his head. I feel a bolt of confidence ripple through me as Malcolm is strapped in. There are teams still rowing on the water so we don't have much of a crowd. The facilitator yells up to the catch and I look over at Malcolm. I know he will win because he is still bubbling with anger. He's got a grudge.

The facilitator is ready and gives them both the nod.

"*Row!*"

Malcolm's machine skips back because he pushes off so hard. Ken and Coach Victor run over and hold down Malcolm's erg because it keeps moving back with every stroke. People are amazed at how strong he is, and I can tell Malcolm is easily beating the other kid by the sound of the fan on his erg. We are all screaming and cheering Malcolm on like crazy, and for the first time I am proud of a teammate. The look on his face says that he's here fighting for something.

He finishes, exhausted, but the other kid is still going. We are all cheering for Malcolm, and he when he gets up he can barely walk or talk he is so drained. He beat his opponent by ten to twelve seconds, a lifetime in a 1,000-meter race. Alvin and Arthur prop him up. The other kid from St. Ignatius stands up and has a look on his face like, *So what, this is only a machine, why are you guys so happy? The water is the real thing.*

I can't focus on him, because now it's my turn. I'm racing the guy who raced on their bow seat. I am on fire with nerves, and it drives me slightly crazy that our opponents appear so calm and perfect. I sit on the machine, close my eyes, and say to myself, *This is precious.* I open my eyes and slide up to the catch, squeeze the handle like a vice grip, and wait for that sound.

"*Row!*"

I drive back with all my power and come back up to the catch at twenty-eight strokes per minute, trying to keep a good pace. I'm breathing hard, and have blocked out all faces and sound. I think about making history, making movies, winning gold medals. I get hit with a wave of sluggishness and open my eyes. I can hear Alvin's voice but I'm not sure what he's saying. I look left at my opponent's face and I can tell he's nervous. He's all alone; it's just him and none of his teammates. Every fight I've had in my life, I have had alone; alone is home for me. I feel comfortable and I grow so confident with every stroke that fatigue starts to leave my body. I row and row and don't look at the clock until Coach Jessica stops me.

"You won."

"I won?" I want to keep going.

I get up and don't make a big deal out of it; I keep my cool and shake my teammate's hands. I don't shake the other guys' hands because they didn't shake ours, but now we feel better about ourselves than we did forty minutes ago. Inside, I'm so winded that I want to collapse.

Coach Jessica lets us know there are snacks in her car and we all run over. Pheodus is still on top of his tree. I yell for him to come down, and he tells me he'll come down when he's ready. Alvin says, "Man, if you put that fool's brain in a bird it would fly backwards."

When we get to the car there are apples and fruit bars. I had never eaten anything healthy until I started rowing and it feels great. The healthy food makes me feel light on my feet. My mind is always clear now and I swear I'm less lazy.

"You missed it, Arshay," Alvin tells me. "Malcolm is going to beat up one of the guys."

"Really? What happened?"

Malcolm says, "One of the guys came up to me saying it's tradition when we lose to give up our shirts. I stepped up to him and said 'come take it,' and he just kind of ran off. I don't care if it is tradition, Mike made us lose."

"Man, Mike is one of the best coaches in the sport," Preston pipes in. "You guys lost that race."

"So I guess our rowing team is more like Michael Jordan going into baseball," I say to Malcolm, and everyone starts laughing.

"More like Charles Barkley going into golf."

"More like Shaq going into movies."

Malcolm laughs. "I deserve that one, but Mike shouldn't have picked our positions." We agree. I know that Mike is the best coach that has taught us, but he just isn't around to see how we're doing. I knew he's legit because he's Coach Jessica's rowing coach. I know that's why she trusted him with us.

We hang by the zoo until Ken and Coach Jessica are finished checking out the other races. She takes Arthur and Pheodus home and Ken takes Alvin, Preston, Malcolm, and me out to dinner somewhere in the West Loop. When we get out of Ken's Jeep there are a lot of really nice restaurants around. I know these places are considered *fine dining*, which I've been learning about in school. The host at the first restaurant tells Ken we can't come in because we aren't dressed for the evening. Ken looks incredulous.

"There are people in there wearing T-shirts and jeans, just like my guys."

"Well, they're not twenty-one."

"Oh? Now it's their age?"

I had a feeling this was going to happen, so we pull Ken away, but he is visibly upset. Malcolm calls the host a "racist bastard" and we walk off.

Ken is not like any other white guy I've ever met. He does what he wants and has a little ghetto in him; he never backs down from anything. We walk down the street until we find a nice place that lets us in. There is something disturbing about thinking that they're being so accommodating just by letting us in. We're good kids, and that seems so backward.

The restaurant is One Sixtyblue, which is owned by Michael Jordan. The service staff is dressed in crisp black and white and they greet us warmly. The host brings us to a beautiful table covered with a white tablecloth with a large candle in the middle. The waiter comes by to introduce himself and gives us each a really big menu. I don't understand a single selection on the menu.

"You in cooking class and you don't understand this?" Preston asks.

"I don't yet, but I will one day. I know the names of six different wines and their colors."

Ken is impressed with that and gives me a high-five.

While I'm looking at my menu it catches on fire because I have it resting on top of the candle. Ken puts it out, and I am mortified. The guys are laughing at our first fine-dining experience and how wrong it's gone already. When the waiter comes back with our water in a wineglass we all start goofing off. We put on "proper" voices, swirl the wineglass, and talk about our experiences at Harvard and Yale. When we notice the prices on the menu we ask Ken if we can have the money instead and just go to Burger King. He laughs and tells us no because life is about experiencing new things.

When the waiter takes our orders, Preston asks for the filet mignon but pronounces it totally wrong. Alvin asks for the New York strip steak, and then asks to substitute the sides for another New York strip steak. The waiter starts laughing, but we don't because we know he is serious. Malcolm and I both play it safe with pasta. It was always a dream of mine to eat at a fancy restaurant. Now that the dream is fulfilled, there is room for more dreams.

Now I want to work at one.

As the sweet sound of jazz fills the room, we laugh and crack jokes about each other while devouring our food. "So what did you guys think about the race today?" Ken asks.

"What race?" Alvin answers, with a massive piece of French bread in his mouth. We all laugh.

"I felt crappy until Eugene talked to me," I say.

"It was straight bogus, but it is what it is," Malcolm adds.

Ken says, "It was the first race, and everyone has a crazy first-race story, and someone always hits that wall every year at the sprints."

"Yeah, it's about bouncing back," Preston says.

I have an inspirational moment and tell the guys, "I feel close to this group and know that the moment we experience pain together, we become a team. We feel the same agony because we care about the same thing."

"Okay, preacher man," Malcolm adds.

"I want you guys to attend the Youth Entrepreneurship class I teach on the West Side once a week," Ken says.

"That's what's up. I can seriously use some cash," Preston replies.

"I will find you guys summer jobs, but how awesome will it be to start your own business?"

"That's what's up," Alvin says.

"Hey, Ken, what happened with the flights, Jordans, clothes, and stuff you said you would give us?" I ask.

"Oh hell, yeah," Malcolm says.

"What?" Ken says in confusion.

"We filled out the paper at the beginning of programming that asked for our shoe size, if we ever been on a plane and stuff," I explain.

Ken laughs. "I never promised anything. I was just curious and wanted to know about you guys."

"Ken and the coaches just said that to get us to stick around, bozos," Preston says confidently.

"I guess it worked," I say, shaking my head left to right.

We all laugh and cheers to that with our glasses of water.

I am grateful to Ken for making all this happen and starting a program that will challenge us. I faced a fear of water and now life is a little less scary. He is a special kind of human being. We respond differently to him than we do to anyone else. We are so used to people we encounter talking *at* us. Nagging us, yelling at us without knowing anything about us. They tell us to do things but don't want to take the time to get to know us. Ken always talks *with* us. He spends time with us, learns our jokes, our ways, our inner strengths and weaknesses. Ken uses his time, talent, and treasure to get to know us.

It's like a bank account: You have nothing to withdraw if you don't make a deposit. A lot of times teachers and parents just want to withdraw from us. They want to know our problems, secrets, and the things that are going on in our lives. They wonder why we never tell them anything, and the reason is because they've never made any deposits. Ken is excellent at making trust and faith deposits in our lives.

10

Moving on Up

Summer moves fast like a flip-book animation, and since the Chicago Sprints, my relationship with Malcolm, Preston, and Alvin has become tighter. When I first started rowing, I didn't care to know much about anyone, but this sport has opened me up to trust. It's a no-brainer that Malcolm bugs the shit out of me, but his debating nature comes from growing up in an apartment with five brothers and three sisters. Malcolm's father is a follower of the Nation of Islam, and most of Malcolm's theories come from his father's mouth. Mama Hawkins, Malcolm's mom, is a sweet elderly woman from the South. She is as spiritual as they come. Malcolm says her spirituality comes from being a victim of so much hate growing up in the racist South. She is excited that he's on the rowing team and not at home stirring up trouble, but we have to deal with him stirring up trouble at the boathouse. Malcolm hinted that his dad doesn't care for Ken because he is Jewish, but you never know the truth with Malcolm. Malcolm is a significant asset to the team, and with his erg scores, he can get into a Division-1 rowing school. That is my hope for him, but the discipline the sport requires scares Malcolm at times.

Alvin is bringing a lot of heart to this team. The same killer mentality he has on the street is the same he brings to this team. When Alvin is on the erg or in the water, he is fighting until his last breath. He is always down for a workout, and I notice when the S.O.A. gang calls his crib to hang out, he comes up with excuses not to. Alvin's dad is happy that he's part of something but is suspicious. His dad is a very old-school kind of guy and asked Alvin and me last week why we were doing this white sport so much. He wonders if Ken is touching us, and we both tell him, "Hell no." Alvin's dad says he doesn't trust Ken because no white man just helps people without expecting anything in return. I want to defend Ken, but Alvin's dad is so scary I don't want to speak up and tell him he's wrong. He is quick-tempered, big, strong, loves his guns, and his kids fear him. I can see Alvin is slowly changing, but it's hard with his dad having that old-school "What I say goes" mentality. Alvin told me once that the crew Philly trip is the best time he's had in his sixteen years of living.

Preston is still all the coaches' favorite. He's the kind of guy that gets everything right the first time, and he is in love with Coach Jessica still. At times she has to remove him from stroke seat because when she steers the boat, the guy can't keep his eyes from her legs. He is a sex addict, along with Alvin, and the girls at school call them serial cheaters.

Malcolm clowns Preston's mom because she always looks like she's smoked forty blunts. Preston's mom sells weed, and I'm sure other things, but it never keeps her from being a disciplined parent. Word got around that Preston's apartment has been raided by the cops a few times, so I stay away. It's sad because he is my oldest friend. I've noticed lately that Preston shows up to practice smelling like weed, and claiming to be Conservative Vice Lords. I am sure it's a phase because he is showing up to practice and going to church with me sometimes.

I am getting more confident every day. Less than a year ago, the highest goal I set for myself was to cook in some fast-food restaurant. Of course, there were dreams of winning the lottery, or becoming a basketball star or rapper. I learned by rowing, visiting Penn, and attending Victory Outreach that this shouldn't be the only dream. I am not the most talented or smartest person on the team or at school, but the practice of a strong work ethic and self-control is helping me to stand out.

Ken and Coach Victor's vision is to develop us as good students academically and not just as athletes. At the end of the school year Coach Victor says, "What good is it to have the fastest boat in the world and not the grades to get into a good college?" Ken spends the summer introducing us to successful black men and women who visit us at the boathouse to share their personal stories and road map to college. The coaches push us to our limits and beyond. Rowing outside of the West Side and at Lincoln Park gives us those moments of being away from the gangs, cops, and zombies, and an opportunity to think clearly.

Ken sets us all up with summer jobs. Alvin and I are working at the Safe Foundation on the West Side, an organization with a mission to keep kids off the street by doing extracurricular activities. We both are camp counselors for third graders. There is something that helps you mature faster when you are placed to help little ones who grew up like you have. Malcolm and Preston are doing handy work in the buildings Ken is rehabbing.

Ken believes in us, but I know that we need to start believing in ourselves, too. I try to challenge my teammates to be better in everything we do. I see the car Ken has, the way he inspires people, the programs he's started, the pictures of his beautiful wife, the large company he owns, and I want a life like that. He is a giant, and I want a seat on his shoulders to see what he sees. I am not sure if Ken understands the impact he is making. You have Malcolm, who rolls with the Gangster Disciples gang, Alvin with S.O.A., and Preston with Conservative Vice Lords, and we are all coming together in one boat, as a team.

We are the only four that are rowing for the summer with Coach Jessica as our coxswain. Summer is not a popular season for youth rowing, so we only hit the water a couple of days a week to stay in shape for the fall. The other teammates are in summer school, working, or chilling until school starts again. We have entrepreneurship class once a week, and I try my best to visit Grace, but she works every day to help her mom pay rent as I do.

I am heading to meet Ken at his home in the West Loop to work out on a Saturday morning, and when I turn onto the 1500 block of Ashland I'm completely blown away. The block looks just like the one from *The Cosby Show*. The houses are all enormous and different shades of brown. The street is filled with bright lights and old antique stones in front of each property. Walking past each place and seeing that these white folks don't have curtains is bugging me out. Inside each home looks medieval. I am not used to walking a street with no cigarette butts, broken glass, or trash. The homes hide the sun, and the tree branches drape right over you. I am at a loss for words but also not surprised that he lives on this gorgeous block.

I ring the doorbell and his wife comes to the door. "Hi, I'm Jeni. Come on in." Jeni is pretty and looks a lot like Jennifer Love Hewitt with the same long dark hair. I can't believe I am meeting the woman behind the man. She is a bit bony and walks like she has the world in the palm of her hand.

Their eighteen-month-old daughter, Winnifred, is crawling around. I'm the first one here, so I play with her for a bit and try to teach her my name. I am in love with their home, a four-story brownstone with chandeliers, a library, and a gym upstairs. Jeni is chilling in the dining room with a book, and once Malcolm, Preston, and Alvin arrive she heads upstairs. I want to thank her for lending her husband to us; in church they always say "behind every good man is a great wife." But I get too nervous to say anything. She seems so tough.

I tell the guys that I don't think she likes us.

"Of course not," Malcolm says, "she's a—"

"—racist," we all say and crack up. He thinks everyone is a racist, so it's not hard to finish his sentences. Malcolm picks up Winnifred.

"And this little one thinks we're aliens!"

Ken tells us it's time to go. When we ask where, he tells us the East Bank Club.

"It's the biggest gym in Chicago. Oprah Winfrey and other celebrities work out there."

"Oprah?"

I tell Preston we have to find Oprah and tell her we're the first black public high school rowing team so we can be on her show. He says okay in a sarcastic voice and everyone starts cracking up.

"Whatever; you guys are dream killers."

When we get to the East Bank Club, it feels like I'm walking into a mall. There are stores, big restaurants, and people everywhere. Ken shows us around the place, upstairs to the huge indoor running track that wraps around the building, and down to the mammoth basketball courts. The main floors have big-screen TVs everywhere, and the men's locker room feels as though I am in an ornate hotel lobby; it is overwhelming.

"Okay, guys," Ken says, "I am going for a run and I want you guys to work on the erg machine and run track."

We nod in agreement, but as soon as he leaves the locker room we run straight to the basketball court. The gymnasium is six times the size of the Manley gym and has several hoop options and basketballs for days. You can see Mr. Clean through the wooden floors and a twinkle on the white walls.

There are some actual Harlem Globetrotters practicing on the court, so we sit and watch them for a few minutes before we start playing. I notice that Alvin isn't much of a basketball player. After a couple games, I try to get some of the guys to go look for famous people with me but they just want to go to the locker room to watch TV. When we walk into the locker room lounge area there are naked old white men everywhere. We've never seen anything like it and are basically vomiting in our shirts.

"Look at that dude's butt," Preston blurts out. "That's nasty."

I am so embarrassed I want to hide in one of the lockers. Hanging out with the older guys from church makes me a little more mature, so I don't goof off as much—but I still can't stop myself from laughing.

When we sit down there are three middle-aged white men in towels watching baseball and chatting. Their conversation is way over our heads. They are talking about hedge funds, investments, country houses, and yachts so Malcolm, Preston, and Alvin start mocking them in their best white-guy voices.

"Hey, Todd Myers, I sent my daughter to Harvard and for crying out loud she dropped out and became an artist."

"Well, Bob Chuckles, for the love of God, she needs a good backhand."

"Fellows, it's really not that bad. I myself lost six million yesterday and my wife left me and took the yacht."

The white guys are turning red in the face trying not to say anything and I can't stop laughing. The guys get up suddenly and mumble something I can't understand, but they are clearly pissed off. Malcolm takes the remote and changes the channel to BET and we sit there to watch. I wish I had the strength to tell the guys to cut it out, but I don't. We are growing as a team but we're still immature in a lot of ways. I know we have to learn how to act and chill out in certain places. In the back of my mind I do have the image of how cool, calm, and collected the rowers from the other teams were. From what I've seen, crew teams are all first class and have a laser focus. They believe in themselves, their backgrounds, and their teammates. I am longing for the day that we become as disciplined but I wonder if we will get there.

After we leave the East Bank Club, we hop into Ken's Jeep Wrangler and he drops us off at home. "What's your top three?" I ask the guys.

"I will go first," Preston insists.

"What's the top three?" Ken asks.

"Not the top three, just top three," I respond.

"It's basically the top three prettiest girls you will want to kick it with," Alvin adds.

"Oh, I see," Ken says.

"Well, number one is Nia Long, two is Stacey Dash, and then Pamela Anderson," Preston says.

"Yes, Pamela Anderson!" Alvin shouts.

"Y'all *would* pick some pink toes," Malcolm adds.

"Okay, you go, Malcolm," I say.

"Ashley Banks from *Fresh Prince*, Tyra Banks, and J.Lo."

"That's a good one," Preston says.

"Okay, I will go," I add. "My number one is Julia Roberts."

"Here we go," Malcolm says, shaking his head.

"Let me go, joe. Julia Roberts, Aaliyah, and Chilli from TLC."

Alvin goes, "I have Oprah, Hillary Clinton, and Pamela Anderson."

"I see Alvin looking for a come up," Preston says. We all laugh.

"What about you, Ken?" Malcolm asks.

"Jeni," Ken answers.

I chuckle, and Malcolm yells, "Lame!"

"Okay, guys," Ken says, demanding our attention. "Have you guys heard of the Head Of The Charles?"

"No," we all say.

"The Head Of The Charles Regatta is the largest two-day rowing event in the world. The energy is fantastic and thousands of people are involved. The best in the world come to compete, and there is a zeal that few in the world will ever experience."

"That's what's up," Malcolm says.

"So how do we race there?" I ask.

"You guys have to train hard and practice at least six days a week."

"Shiiit," Preston adds.

Ken goes on, saying, "It's a three-mile race, and I would love to see you guys there one day.

"It's a nonstop power race," he says, "moving in sync with seven other guys in the same motion for twenty minutes with no breaks whatsoever."

Even though I tell Ken that I've gone a day without eating, been in fistfights, beaten with belts and cords, tackled on a football field, and hit upside the head with a glass bottle and none of it hurts more than a 2,000-meter race on an erg machine when you're giving your all, the truth is, I can only imagine this. I ask Ken why rowing is never on sports channels or in local papers.

"I guess people don't consider it exciting," Ken says with a shrug.

"Well," I say, "once everyone sees the Head Of The Charles Regatta, maybe they will change their minds. Men love seeing women in tights, and I'm sure ladies love seeing men in tights. People love being by the water, it's a great family event, there's no blood, and to see the waves and splashing of water is beautiful."

I can tell the other guys are getting annoyed with my rambling, but Alvin says, "I love how the coxswain is screaming and yelling to motivate the guys on the boat. I would be cursing everyone out."

Hearing about racing in Boston is fascinating to me; it's like hearing about the Holy Land. Most people will only dream about it. Racing in the Head Of The Charles Regatta becomes a goal for me, and I'm hoping my ambition will be contagious to my teammates.

Driving from downtown Chicago only a few miles to the West Side is like night and day. The city is like the water in the lagoon; the outside is crystal clear and clean, but deep inside are all sorts of horrible things that will scare the bejesus out of you. We are a block away from Alvin's place, at the stop sign on Albany Street. There are at least ten guys from the S.O.A. gang, standing there on the corner wide eyeing the Jeep. Black kids rolling up with a white dude is something I bet they don't see every day.

One guy says, "Alvin, you not riding with *The People*, right?"

Alvin shakes his head no, but they still seem confused. I ask Alvin why they call the cops *The People,* but Ken answers.

"Arshay, if you go to court today, the case will be called *The People versus Arshay Cooper.* It's you against the system."

Ken has dropped everyone else off and now we are heading to my crib. I hope he doesn't ask to come in to use the restroom or anything. He's met everyone else's family many more times than mine. The team jokes that I don't really have a home because I never let them in, but my apartment is so small. I'm sure the guys wouldn't mind, they will crack jokes no matter the size. The guys say I'm becoming less hood every day. Malcolm always calls my mom Sister Betty Shabazz because all she does is go to church when she is not working. My stepdad, Ike, went into the home but left a week later and started back on drugs.

I really believe that people don't understand how much I learned from watching *Family Matters, The Fresh Prince of Bel-Air,* and *A Different World.* Dwayne Wayne's character taught me that no matter how hard school gets or no matter what people say about your physical appearance, push through it and be yourself, and always give back to the place that gave to you. Steve Urkel's character taught me how to love a girl and the importance of patience. *The Fresh Prince of Bel-Air* demonstrated how to be a good son, and even if you are without a father, there is still a bright future that lies ahead. I practice everything I learn from these shows in my daily life and I get positive results.

Five minutes before we arrive at my place, Ken asks, "How did you get to where you are today?" I want to say *church.* "Ken, I learned from TV what is missing in my life: a trusted teacher, a father figure, a mentor, friends that are positive and loyal. I decided to seek those missing pieces because they aren't necessarily around me. I joined a team of brothers, I go to church on my own time to hang with positive influences, and I hang around you."

"Wow," Ken says.

I ask if I can go to his place tomorrow to chill and learn more about rowing. He tells me I can if I will help him clean out his garage. I jump out of Ken's car, ecstatic just daydreaming about what's to come in the future, and I believe that I will lead this team as captain.

The next morning, when I get to Ken's place, he's upset because someone stole his bike from his garage.

"From here? This is a nice neighborhood."

"Yeah, *this* is where they go to steal. No one is going into the inner city to steal someone's bike, because they are most likely shitty or belong to someone who will bust a cap in your ass."

We decide to go for a run and Ken has me chill with Winnifred while he goes to find workout clothes for me. I play with Winnifred for a few minutes and I'm shocked when she remembers my name; she is a very smart baby. She is so cute and only crawls with one hand. I pick her up and toss her in the air and she starts crying and I realize she isn't the type of kid that likes physical play. She's a little fancy.

When Ken comes down he says, "Did you pinch my daughter?"

"No, man, I didn't!"

"Arshay, I'm kidding," he says, laughing at me.

I let out a sigh of relief. "Come on, man, you can't play like that."

Ken yells upstairs to Jeni that he's leaving and she yells back that he should bring Winnifred upstairs.

"Hey, Jeni," I yell up to her.

She says hello back in a strange tone. I can't help but think that this woman does NOT like me.

I change clothes and Ken and I head out on our run. We pass Malcolm X College, United Center, Crane High School, and head toward the Rockwell Gardens projects. There are a few guys standing outside; I'm not sure if they are selling drugs or just hanging out. It is early so I assume they are selling drugs. This is about the same time the guys from my hood start.

As we run past them, one says, "Look at this cracker." His buddies start laughing.

I know that we're near the projects, so the best plan is just to keep it moving, but Ken stops running. I see him walk back to the guy and say, "Come on, man, I'm just going for a run."

The guy is looking at Ken like he just lost his mind. I think to myself, *It is too hot and early for this madness.*

"Who you talking to?" The guys laugh again.

I have seen this scene too many times; Ken is going to get jumped if he doesn't chill out.

"Ken, let's go," I say.

"Get your homie," one of the guys says to me. They think it's funny and I can't tell if Ken is playing around.

The guy steps down, though. "My bad, man, it's all good."

He holds out his hand and Ken shakes it.

Ken gives him a nod and starts running again. I want to tell him how stupid that was, but I keep my mouth shut. Ken is completely fearless, and I keep wondering where he gets his confidence or his pent-up craziness.

One time, about a week after our first race, Ken takes us to the University of Illinois at Chicago to go bowling and all the pins get stuck. So he walks down the bowling lane to line up the pins himself while we are yelling that he can't do that. The staff is even yelling that he can't do that, but Ken does what he wants when he wants. With Ken and the team hanging out a lot, we notice things that white people can do that black people can't get away with.

When we get back to Ken's place after the run, we start working on the garage. I hand him random things while he stands on the ladder nicely stacking them on the new shelving unit he just purchased. He spends some time talking about college rowing. "What do you think it takes to get more kids at school rowing?" I ask.

"Good question. It will probably take you talking to them, Arshay."

"Me?"

"Yeah. We provided money, vision, and coaches. We just need the connection."

"I am not popular though."

"But you're passionate. If you can get freaking Preston and Alvin to go to church, you can get kids to row."

"True, and if I can get Malcolm to go to church, then I can get kids to win medals." We both start laughing.

He tells me how he wants to retire from trading sooner rather than later and spend his life teaching and building Urban Options. He says to me that a career is fantastic, "but there is no higher calling than helping kids and giving back." I ask a lot of questions about starting a business and he tells me what he knows and even offers to print out some articles that will help me.

"I want to be a chef, Ken."

"My friend is a cook."

"Not a cook. A cook is employed in a chef's kitchen. I want to be a chef, but not a regular one, a traveling chef or something."

"Let me know what you need to get there," Ken says. "Just keep taking my entrepreneurship classes. How are your grades?"

"They're okay." I shrug. "I just have an issue staying focused. All I think about is rowing or Grace."

"Those are not bad thoughts but sometimes it is good to have tunnel vision."

"What's tunnel vision?"

"Tunnel vision is focus," he explains. "Limiting what you see or think. When you're in a tunnel you can only go one way. When you're in school, think about school. When you're with Grace, think about Grace. When you're rowing, think about rowing."

"Wow. That helps, because my mind is always all over the place."

Ken tells me he taught a class at Manley and met Grace. "She is a sweetie pie."

"I know, but I don't think I have a shot."

"Patience is a virtue, Arshay."

I ask Ken about Jeni, and tell him I don't think she likes us very much. "Does she think we're freeloaders or something?"

"No, not at all. Jeni is a firecracker who takes nada from no one, and she's also busy with law school."

"How is she a firecracker?"

Ken laughs aloud. "Where do I start?"

He tells me about a time that they went to the movies in North Lawndale. While they were in the theater, Jeni got up to use the restroom. About ten minutes passed and he heard some screaming and yelling outside the theater and knew it was her. When he stepped out, there was security everywhere and Jeni was charging three black women. One of the girls had been beating her kid in the bathroom and Jeni told her to stop.

"Damn! She is a G."

"I love her," he says. "She is a unique individual who never backs down. We're both fearless and we understand the world the same way. She's going to be a criminal defense attorney, and she will be the best at it."

I stay over late and have dinner with Ken, Jeni, and Winnifred. We bond and Jeni explains to me what *criminal defense* means, and about the job she'll be doing. I tell Jeni about Grace and how I think that even if I get to be with her I know I won't know what to do.

"What do you mean?" she asks.

"Grace is smarter, very good looking, and she's *been* dating. I just don't know how to entertain her or be a cool boyfriend."

"You're insecure. There is no reason to be insecure." Ken tells her to relax, but she keeps going. "No, don't tell me to relax. Arshay, there is no reason to be insecure. You go get what you want."

Just like that, she gets up from the table and heads toward the stairs.

"I have to get some work done."

Ken looks across the table at me.

"Welcome to my world."

On the drive home, I tell Ken something that no one but my mom knows.

"When I was in eighth grade, I didn't pass the state test to make it to high school. I was supposed to make a 6.8 reading and math level to pass." I take a deep breath.

"Things were so messed up at home that I couldn't even read a paragraph without thinking about how bad life was. I was so focused on how to be cool for the kids at school that I couldn't focus on adding numbers. I would have a painful night and then go to school the next morning and have to read some bland fiction.

"I messed up that test on purpose by turning it in when everyone else did to not seem dumb. I didn't even try. So I failed, but they let me walk across the stage. They told me I had to go to summer school for the bridge program and I could go to high school if I passed, but I also failed the test in summer school. Not because I purposely failed, but because I felt like I wasn't smart enough. I tried, but my mind was always elsewhere. So I was told I had to repeat the eighth grade and if I did well by Christmas break they would place me in high school.

"This all happened right around the time my mom graduated from the recovery home. I was so embarrassed that all the friends that I hung out with, laughed with, and fought alongside would be going to high school without me. I felt even dumber. So I told my mother to transfer me to an elementary school far away so we could move out of the neighborhood. I purposely lost contact with every single friend at William

Penn just so I could focus. I didn't really forgive them for making my life hell anyway. So with no friends around I was able to focus and learn. Hanging with some church guys every once in a while helped, too. I read my first book, *The Count of Monte Cristo*. That was a big accomplishment for me.

"After that, I passed with flying colors and went back to my correct grade. I believe it's a combination of my mom getting her act together and me making a choice to trade in fun for my future."

Ken is amazed. He tells me he is proud of me and says I will be a good team captain one day. I get out of the car but turn back.

"Just one more thing."

"What's that?"

"How much was the check you gave that lady for the bus cr—"

"Get out of here!"

I'm cracking up as I head inside, happier and more confident than I've ever been. Ken is undoing what all the bad teachers and friends did to my self-esteem. Watching his actions and seeing the man he is to his family gives me hope.

I think about Ken and all the things I used to go through at home, and how nobody knew. I think about how I wasn't really alone, that it's possibly happening to every young man and woman I know in my school and in my city. My mind is filled with voices that I've heard in the last year from the guys at church, the guys at the barbershop, my mom, and Ken. Those voices are talking about change and the responsibility of reaching out to those who are hurting. I want to be an agent of change for my teammates and those around me but I feel a little bit like I have one foot in and one foot out because I'm still young and want to be cool. But in the hood, the cemetery is full of young guys who wanted to be cool. For my crew, it has been the best summer of our lives. Sadly, we have to live in a community of neglect, chaos, and distrust, but if we can hang in there like we hang at the catch, we will build the strength to help us maintain.

II

Captain

Summer has come to an end, and we are one week out before race day at the St. Louis regatta. Nerves are flying high between the guys and school starting back in two days doesn't help. I am sitting at the desk, drawing oars and waiting for youth entrepreneurship class to start. Urban Options hosts the program at the Center for Youth on the West Side. There are at least twenty kids in the class from different sports programs. Ken teaches the class one day a week, and sometimes he will have a guest facilitator. It's a pretty tight space with rectangular tables, blue plastic chairs, and a monster chalkboard. Anxiety must be eating away at Alvin, Malcolm, and Preston, considering I haven't heard a sound from them since I've been sitting at the desk. I feel like I missed my window of opportunity that night after we left Grace's place to talk to Alvin about his dad because when I mentioned it to him the other day, he shut it down quickly. Or he just moved on, given that a different problem arises every day on the West Side. Preston is dressing super flashy, and I am dying to know if Big Cliff is buying him gear. I saw that Big Cliff dropped him off today. Malcolm taps me and says, "I need to come up with a lie, bruh."

"Why?"

"My old man doesn't want me doing this rowing shit."

"Get the hell out of here," I say in shock.

"My dad doesn't trust whites, bruh. On the real."

"Ken's cool."

"Ken's white."

"We do have a crappy history with them," Preston adds.

"My family been through so much in the South, ain't no forgiving," Malcolm says.

"What about your mom?" I ask.

"Oh, my mom loves Ken."

"Well, there you go."

"Arshay, you don't have a dad in the house, so you don't know how this shit work," Malcolm pleads.

"Here we go again," I say.

Alvin sits quiet, and Ken walks in to start class. I tell Malcolm we will come up with something because we race in a week.

Ken opens up the class by asking everyone to throw out their business idea. He then talks about the marketplace, the economy, and asks us what business we think our community needs. When we answer specific questions correctly, he throws us a nutrition bar. The class keeps getting better by the week. Ken teases Malcolm a little bit because during our last lesson we brainstormed business ideas, and Malcolm said we should take muffins and put frosting on them to sell.

"Fool, that's a cupcake," Alvin said. Ken couldn't stop laughing about it.

Toward the end of class, Ken takes out a twenty-dollar bill and asks who wants it. Everyone starts calling out.

"I'll ask again, who wants this?"

Everyone yells louder, "I do!" while raising their hands.

Ken screams, "Who wants this?"

When Ken looks at me, I just know he would give it to me. I need it. Everyone screams louder until one student jumps up and grabs the bill out of Ken's hands. He smiles.

"See? If you want it, you can't just yell and talk about it. You have to get up and go get it, period."

Damn, this really got me because I could use that twenty bucks and the lesson was on point. As young people, we shout to the rooftop that we want to go to college, make the NBA, graduate high school, win a race, or get a job. Those things will never come to pass if we sit on our butts and just say we want it. We have to get up, put in the work, and get it because if we don't someone will take what is supposed to be ours, like that twenty dollars.

We head to Ken and Jeni's place, where I grill some chicken breasts and Jeni sautés some mixed veggies. When I walk upstairs to make the call for dinner, I notice that there is a huge painting on the wall of us rowing in the lagoon, and Ken tells us Jeni got it for him for his birthday.

"This is nice," Malcolm says, "but they're black faces with white-face features." Alvin starts laughing, and I tell them to shut up about it even though Malcolm is right. Ken runs in another room and comes back. "Guys, I forgot to tell you about this!" In his hands is an article from the *Pennsylvania Gazette*.

"It's about the rowing team," he says. I quickly snatch it from his hand. "Another article to put on the wall," I tell the guys.

"You thirsty," Malcolm says.

I walk downstairs reading it while the guys beg for it. It's an alumni profile about Ken and his efforts titled SCULLING FOR SUCCESS.

We sit at the table to eat and begin talking about the violence in Chicago. Jeni is always looking to start a great conversation when we come over. *She would be one kick-ass school teacher,* I think to myself.

"One of the leading causes of violence in this city is because the community doesn't trust the Chicago Police Department, so they seek revenge themselves," Jeni tells us. She continues to adds her two cents on the lack of trust between CPD and the West Side and speaks highly of the Chicago Innocence Project. "I remember when the cops kicked Pookie G.," Malcolm says. "It was horrible."

"All of us have gotten smacked around by cops for being black," Preston adds.

I just sit quiet, pondering my experience and thinking about Pookie getting kicked.

"Well, I would've snapped," Malcolm says.

Preston gives him a look. "No, you wouldn't."

"Don't ever talk back to the cops," Jeni warns us, "especially as young black men. Don't be intimidated, but be smart and do what they say. You won't win. That's a rule." We nod, and I tell the guys it might be better if we had local softball and basketball games for cops and the guys in the neighborhood to play together.

"Or if they came to block parties and school games to hang out, they might build some trust then."

"That will never happen," Alvin says, shaking his head. I know he's right. I've been getting stopped by police since I was a kid. No block party is going to change that.

"I do think that some cops would like to build a relationship with our community, but they get the sense that they're the enemy and hold back. And I guess we do think they're enemy, so it's just crazy. Remember when Ken dropped us off at Alvin's?" I say. "The guys in the neighborhood thought we were riding with *The People*. It made us look like we can't be trusted."

"Exactly," Malcolm agrees. "Being friends with cops will get us killed."

When it comes time for us to head home, Ken gives us thirty dollars and puts us in a yellow cab. We get in the taxi, and our eyes bug out when we see that the meter is already two dollars. Once we're around the corner, we have the cab driver let us out. He gets upset and tells us to get the hell out. We get out laughing, split the money four ways, and head toward the train.

I get off the train reflecting on all we discussed at Ken and Jeni's. I reach my place and take a seat on the stoop. My heart feels heavy think-ing about my community, and being on the water is usually best when I have this feeling. The relationship between those who serve and pro-tect and my community is nonexistent. I don't know what it is like to be the child of a cop who hopes that their parent makes it home safe after working in a community I am afraid to walk in. I don't want to hate cops, because I remember when my grandfather was abusive to my granny, and they showed up and removed him when no one else would. I don't know how tough it is to be them. I know what it is like to be me. Amidst this chaos on the West Side, I have never sold drugs, punched, shot, or disrespected anyone in any way. I mean, I haven't even broken a plate, and I still had my face pressed down on a police car numerous times. It's not fun when they stick their hands down your pants, looking for drugs. Once, when an officer took my backpack and flipped it upside down and made me pick my books up, I had so much on my mind. I wanted to tell the cop that I recited the preamble to the United States Constitution in front of my whole class with pride. One night I cried myself to sleep because I couldn't remember the Declaration of Independence for my eighth-grade history class. I wanted to tell the cop that I put my right hand on my chest, took my hat off, and sang the national anthem at my first baseball game with goose bumps.

I pledge allegiance to the flag, I help old ladies cross the street, and I work with kids. I want to stand up for myself, but any wrong move can scare him and get me killed, then what? What will they say about me? That I am on the crew team or I live on the West Side? What picture will they show? Me holding an oar or the one with my hat turned backward? Will I get a flag on my casket or cheap drugstore roses? I am scared, too. Most joes will flee in this situation. When a kid is penalized for being black and walking, you think just to lie or run from the police. It doesn't mean you're guilty. I should have told that cop that I am American! But when you are advised to shut your mouth from the cops and your peers, there is no hope to see through each other's eyes. At the Victory Outreach homes, they preach a lot about accountability. I think that word is the answer. If black people hold other black people accountable for killing their own, things may change, and I am slowly seeing them speak out in our local events. If white people speak out against other white people about racism, that helps this country. I am noticing this happening in the media. What I have not seen yet is cops marching against other police officers that mistreat blacks. When that happens, I believe then we are moving toward change.

Today I wake up before the alarm clock goes off. It was a tossing-and-turning kind of night. I walk into the kitchen, pop on my mom's worship CD, and begin to pray for safety on the first day of school. I pray that I will stay rooted in all that I've learned this summer and for a successful rowing season.

When I arrive at Manley, I can feel the excitement in the air. The freshman girls are jumping rope, students are chillin' on the trunks of cars, vibing off Chicago house music, and the gangs are just posted up on the corners minding their own. Usually, this would be a busy morning for cops and security, but today is different.

It is time for our practice meeting and it is great to see that Pookie G., Malcolm's nephew, transferred over to Manley just to be on the crew team. I can hear a loud, raspy voice that sounds like Chris Tucker coming from the hall, and now into the room.

This tall and scraggy kid with nappy hair and a big birthmark on the right side of his temple comes in and sits on the teacher's desk. "What's up niggas and niggettes?"

Everyone is laughing.

"Guess who's coming over tonight?" he asks Elliot.

"Who?"

"These nuts!" he shouts, cracking himself up.

I decide to make my presence known.

"What's up, my brother?"

He looks over at me, scanning from my shoes to my head as if I shouldn't have spoken to him.

"You not my *brotha* until you've drunk suga water."

Alvin looks confused. "You mean *sugar* water?"

"No, I mean suga water."

Alvin asks if he's some kind of comedian or something, but I tell him it's cool. Everyone is laughing at this guy or laughing with him. I'm not sure.

"Man," I tell him, "I've had plenty of suga water."

"Not Kool-Aid, just water and suga."

I nod. "With every meal."

"The black-kid struggle," he says, reaching for my hand. "I guess you my brotha."

I shake his hand and instantly feel a connection. I saw this kid last year on the freshman side of the building telling jokes to the gamers, and they were pissing in their pants. He is now a sophomore.

"Dude," Alvin says in disbelief, "you just drunk straight sugar in water?"

"Yeah, man, all the time. You have to try it."

"Hell to the naw."

I look back at the kid, and he is already cracking jokes to some girl. I walk over.

"Hey, my name is Arshay."

"I'm Josh, and why you all up on me, man? Can I breathe?"

Everyone laughs again, and I'm hoping he isn't another Malcolm.

Coach Jessica comes in, and I notice that Preston and Malcolm aren't here yet. Coach Jessica asks me about them, but I tell her I don't know.

"Okay, guys, listen up. First thing: Coach Victor is no longer with us."

"What? Why?" I ask.

"He decided to move on," she replies. I feel hurt. When a coach leaves, you start to think right away it is your fault or did he get fired. Like, why make an impact on someone's life and bounce? Preston and Malcolm stroll in.

"Glad you decided to join us," Coach Jessica says.

"Yo, Coach Victor is gone," I tell them.

"He dead?" Malcolm asks.

"No, idiot, another job," I answer.

"I am not surprised; y'all bad," Preston says.

"Okay guys, fall silent," Coach Jessica demands.

"For those who are new, we row in a sport called crew. It's pretty much always been a white sport, but you guys add something new and fresh."

Josh says, "Like flavor."

"There are a few people here from last year's team who raced and will be racing next week in St. Louis." Everyone claps and shouts they want to go.

"That race is set, but you guys will travel to Iowa this month if you trained hard and show up."

Coach Jessica writes on the board and says this year we will spend time talking about the team culture, racing goals, and academics. She goes on to explain, then shouts, "Special announcement! Arshay is our new captain." Everyone shouts and whistles in celebration. I am at a loss for words. I have come so far; I thank God in my silence.

"Arshay, you have demonstrated leadership, perseverance, and commitment. Please stand and say a few things."

Everyone turns to look at me.

"Yes, rowing is unique to me. There are days when you feel like it's your time, like the best of your talents is just about to materialize, that you're on the verge of history. Then there are days when you feel like you don't belong and you should do everyone a favor and crawl back into your mom's womb. The good news is you change for the better."

"I've changed," Alvin says, nodding.

Elliot jumps in. "Me, too."

Everyone starts clapping and I feel amazing after speaking. I want to make a difference; I feel like it's our year. All I know is the water is my peace. I live in a place where I have been taught not to swim in deep water, to always wear a life jacket when I'm in a boat. I feared the water and any sport that had to do with water. Now, when I'm in the boat, I don't hear gunshots or ambulance sirens. I don't see gang signs and I don't have fear because Alvin is behind me and Preston is in front of me. I feel powerful.

"One more announcement," Coach Jessica says while opening a big brown box.

"Malcolm, Alvin, Preston, Arshay, and Elliot, come up to get your uniforms for this week's race." Another roar of celebration happens. She pulls out these black Manley Crew hoodies and matching sweatpants that have *Manley* printed on them with red oars framing the top and bottom. For racing, we have short cotton black shorts and the T-shirt is white, red, and black and reads *Manley Crew*. I am not crazy about the shorts, but I love everything else. I am ready to hit the water.

Coach Jessica tells the students attending the info session that they, too, will receive uniforms when they are committed. Practice will be every day after school with homework help during the first half hour of practice at the lagoon until the winter and then back to the school gym on ergs. I'm still in shock about Coach Victor's exit, but Coach Jessica assures us that we will find another coach and it is posted all over the *Rowing News* magazine. When she dismisses the group, Josh jumps up.

"See you fools later, and maybe I will be back."

Preston, Malcolm, Alvin, and I hop into Coach Jessica's Jeep to head to practice at the lagoon.

We arrive and get right into our routine. We change our clothes, stretch, take a jog around the lagoon, take out the oars, grab the boat, check the seats and foot stretcher, get on the water, and push off. I am having a hard time focusing because St. Ignatius Loyola Academy is on the water and rowing picture-perfect. I'm not sure if they have better coaching, they train on their own outside of practice, or if they have newer boats, but they're fast.

"Arshay!" Coach Jessica screams from the cox seat. "Keep your head in the boat."

I know I have to get out of my head. I just want to prove to everyone in this sport that we belong here. Preston has to work on relaxing on the slide and setting the perfect pace as a stroke seat, Malcolm on his cardio, Alvin on less pulling and more pushing, and I need better flexibility to have a long drive. Power is never an issue for us, but that's what we depend on. Today's practice is about bridging and connecting to the oar, water, boat, and ourselves. I feel ready for St. Louis.

It's the end of the week and me and Alvin are walking to school and I can't wait until the school day is over so we can drive to St. Louis. When the final bell rings, we run outside and jump in Coach Jessica's car. Coach Jessica's friend Mandy from her rowing team is there as well, so Alvin, Malcolm, and I ride with Mandy, and Preston rides with Coach Jessica. We say Preston is "living the dream" and start laughing.

"Malcolm, your dad let you come?"

"Yeah, man, my mom and he fought about it, but I'm here."

"Thank God."

"Don't thank him yet; let's see what happens for the next one."

It's a long six-hour drive. On the road we see other rowers with stickers on their cars and some trucks with boats on top. We're reminded that this is a big event. "Hey, guys, what books are you reading in school?" Mandy asks.

"We just started school, but I read a book this summer called *Treasure Out of Darkness*, that was pretty uplifting. This guy at church pays the young people twenty dollars to read these books of his choice and ask a few questions."

"That's why you read?" Malcolm asks.

"Naw dude, it's just motivation."

"I read the newspaper every day," Alvin adds. Mandy recommends books we should read.

When we get to St. Louis we get dinner and then check into our hotel to rest. Once we're unpacked, the guys start getting the pre-race jitters. I remind them that if we win this race we will make the papers again. They all agree with me and say they feel ready.

We're all in shock the next morning when we see how beautiful the Creve Coeur lake is. It's breathtaking, and the water seems five times the size of the lagoon. The trees are lime green, and the water is crystal clear. On one part of the lake, people are paddle boarding and kayaking, and on the trail, folks are rollerblading and biking. It's much bigger than the race we had in Chicago. It is amazing to me that all rowers seem the same: tall and lean with beautiful bone structures. Everyone is representing their team colors on their spandex. We are all sporting our Manley racing shirts but with basketball shorts and headbands. We decided to not wear the small cotton shorts. There are a lot of people stretching and hanging out until their race time, so we walk around checking out the lady rowers. Everyone is looking at us and we are turning countless heads. We walk past a guy with bright orange hair interviewing a team with a tape recorder.

Alvin yells out, "Don't you want to interview the black oarsmen?"

Preston tells Alvin to chill.

"Guys, let's just race and get out of here," I tell them.

Malcolm shrugs. "I'm here for the experience. We're not about to win any races."

"Don't be a dream killer," I say.

. . .

Malcolm and Preston split off. Alvin sings to every girl he sees and they smile and keep walking. I walk over to the dock to check out some of the cool boats I saw on the way down. I wish that I knew more about this world; everything is so foreign and water is something we've always been told to stay away from. I reread the *Chicago Tribune* article about us almost every day, and what sticks out the most is when the writer says we are "dipping our toes into very foreign waters." Every time I practice, and before I get into the boat, I say to myself, "Okay, this is foreign water."

While admiring the boats, I hear someone approaching me. It is the reporter that Alvin was trying to get to interview us. He has a small recorder, so I figure he isn't really legit. He asks if I have a second and I say sure, but my coach is just outside the boathouse.

"It's okay, just a few questions." He puts the tape recorder near my face. I can see Alvin walking over.

"So, they say the black oarsmen will change the sport?" He must have heard Alvin when we said we are the black oarsmen.

I just stare at him because I'm not sure if he's serious or sarcastic.

"No, we're just changing our lives."

"Is this your first race? And are you nervous?"

"No . . . and no."

"What makes your team different from everyone else?"

I blink at him while holding in a loud laugh, and then slowly look around at every other rowing team there. I say into the recorder, "We wear headbands."

Alvin is cracking up and the reporter just nods his head.

"Does your team have any goals?"

"Hopefully we win, and make history."

He thanks me and walks off.

Alvin shouts after him, "What about my interview?"

"Next time," the reporter yells back.

Alvin tells me that all my time with Victory Outreach has made me quick with my speech.

"Nah, man, I've just been dealing with people talking trash all my life."

As we walk away, it occurs to me what we've been missing. I think the problem is that we don't talk more about personal goals on the team; we're just going day by day. I know the overall goal is to race in Michigan in the spring and to be winners outside the boat, but we also need our own personal goals. My mother always says people perish without vision. I think that applies to our team, too. I'm a true believer that if you have a bow and arrow and aim for nothing, you will hit nothing every time. We need a clear target, a clear goal. Ken talked to me about vision before, and having the ability to focus on what you want and then get it.

Closer to race time the weather changes. It is cloudy and a little wind picks up. There are even waves on the lake, but it doesn't look too scary after watching the previous races. Coach Jessica tells us to take a knee on the grass.

"Guys, we've had some good practices. Remember it's about drive and recovery on the boat: drive back with power and recover on the way up. When you recover correctly, you will have a powerful drive. There are some waves out there, so I want you to concentrate on full, powerful strokes and timing. I don't want you guys catching a crab out there."

There is no time to think about all of that now, because it's time to row. We pick up the boat and walk toward the lake with the boat over our shoulders. We have our game faces on, and people stop what they're doing to see us row. I can see the interviewer watching us, and when I make eye contact he gives me a wink. I'm not sure if he is on our side or just thinks we're a joke.

When we place the boat down into the water there are three other teams out there. More and more teams come over to watch, but I don't mind because I know we're something different to the rowing world. I'm also happy that no one in our boat has a lifejacket on. Ken isn't here with us, so I feel a little strange, or alone, I guess. I brush the feeling aside.

We push off to the starting line and I tell myself, *It's our time.* The waves are strong, so it takes a little time to properly set up at the starting line. Preston is back in stroke seat, Malcolm is in seat three, I'm in two, and Alvin is in bow. I look over to size up our opponents but Coach Jessica is ordering us to the catch. We reach forward as far as we can. I see that the other teams are at the finish, as if they just finished a stroke.

"*Row!*"

We take off. We are racing neck and neck with everyone. I can feel the boat moving as fast as it ever has. The waves are getting stronger and the boat is rocking up and down with water splashing everywhere. Alvin starts screaming as he's rowing.

"There's water getting into the boat!"

"We're gonna flip!" I yell to Coach Jessica.

"Keep going, don't stop this damn boat!"

Preston yells out that he's getting hit with waves, and we continue complaining while rowing. Coach Jessica is screaming her head off.

"My shorts are stuck to the seat!" I yell out.

"Keep rowing, guys. This is it!"

In all the intensity, I am having trouble taking full strokes. My forearm is throbbing, there are blisters all over my hands, and the oar is slippery. There are no timeouts or breaks in rowing, so I bash on, taking extra care to make sure that my blade gets into the water at the same time as the others blades to avoid a crab. There is no more quit in me. I have felt pain all my life; it's my *normal.*

Two boats are ahead of us, but not by much, and before I can figure out how we're doing we are across the finish line and in third place. We fold over our legs in exhaustion. Alvin taps my shoulder.

"We didn't get last!"

"I know."

"Not bad, guys," Coach Jessica says, "but it could have been better. Now you see, Arshay, that's why you wear spandex, so your shorts won't get stuck."

All the guys agree that, stuck or not, we're never wearing spandex but will do the short cotton ones, and she laughs and gives up.

We get off the boat and tip it up and water comes pouring out. I'm not happy with our results, but I'm happy that we finished. I can't wait to see Ken and talk about setting team goals and how to become better. I am ready for this leadership role. On every team, you will find someone who wants it more than everyone else. On the Bulls it was MJ. He was not satisfied with wanting it more than everyone but understood if you can get the team to have the same will to win that you have, success happens. The guys on the team always tease me, telling me to slow down, that I get too excited. I know I get ahead of myself sometimes, so I decide to live my life the way I race on the boat and the erg.

It's all about *drive* and *recovery*.

12

Dry Tears

Monday mornings suck, today especially. I am late for school and beat the hell up from the St. Louis regatta. After a race, your whole body starts to malfunction, particularly your back. I hate being tardy, so I am speed walking in pain to school. Approaching the school, I see a few of the ex-ballplayers from Manley hanging out on the corner. They all look awful. Only a few years ago these guys were star athletes making the local paper, with real potential to get into a Division 1 college, bigger colleges with the best reputations and televised athletics. They are probably only about twenty years old, but they look forty. Their clothes are too big, their hair is uncombed, their eyes are bloodshot, and their lips are jet black from smoking blunts. My heart bleeds for them and it bothers me because some of the ballplayers in my class are heading down the same road.

I blame some of the teachers and coaches for this. It seems like the only responsibility the basketball players have is to give 100 percent when it comes to winning. Everything else is given to them, like good grades, new shoes, girls, individual attention, and protection. Guys like me have to earn all of that. Maybe that's a good thing because the players that aren't good enough to get scholarships seem to fall apart quickly. When you work extra hard through high school and earn every grade, it's easier to resist the nonsense of the streets. I feel like the coaches develop them too much as athletes and not as good human beings. It's almost as if their existence is about basketball skills and not life skills. I realize now why all the traveling, classes, mentoring, and exposure was more of a priority than rowing. If this program were shut down, I know exactly what I want to do next.

On my way to class I hear Josh, with his raspy voice. I see him over by the stairs, telling jokes to an audience. He is magnetic. I have to get him alone and try to sell him on becoming a rower.

I walk over and poke his back and he turns around like he's about to strike.

"Boy, get your paws off me." I laugh and he squints at me. "Do I know you?"

"Come on, man, you know me."

"You been eating Cheetos?"

Everyone starts laughing, and I say, "Dude, my breath doesn't smell. Listen, man, we're going on the water tomorrow to row, we can use you."

"Use me? Only women can use me."

I'm frustrated because he won't stop joking, so I just nod at him and walk away.

"Arshay." I turn around to hear him out. "See you tomorrow."

"Cool."

I can tell Josh is the kind of guy who will clown you so bad you will want to hide in a closet. I do not doubt that he will be a comedian someday. Josh is also the type of kid who, when he sees someone throwing a rock, he will pick up one and try to throw it farther. He is hungry, anxious, and searching for something. I am geeked to have him.

Coach Jessica and Ken want me and the guys to recruit, so I am looking for those who didn't make the basketball and football teams. Manley is also full of kids that will play video games all night long until they win. I am looking for that student. Crew is all about taking these young people who are misfits in their school and have no coordination and making them into top rowing athletes. Next on my list is Dwayne.

Dwayne is this bony, tall kid who can sing his butt off. All he seems to care about is music. He has a good heart and doesn't belong to any team. Alvin chased him early last year to beat him up but, boy, he was Jesse Owens fast. So, this is going to be a strange pitch. I realize being a captain is a critical responsibility, and it's my job to take some of the load off the coaches.

When I get to lunch, I see Alvin, Pookie G., Malcolm, Elliot, and Preston sitting at the table. I go and sit with Dwayne.

"What's up homie?" I say.

"Arshay, what brings you to this table?"

"I want you to bust a note."

"We sing after school on the stoop by the main door, come then."

"I will, but I want to talk to you about the crew team."

"I thought about it, but that's not for me," he says, eating a super donut.

"Listen, Dwayne, in less than a year I've been to Wisconsin, Philly, St. Louis, and I'll be going to Iowa soon. I ate in the fanciest restaurants and met all kinds of people. Only crew can do that for a high schooler. If you join the team, imagine how many people will hear your voice."

"Damn, really?" Dwayne says.

"Really. We need you, bruh."

"I will race once and see what it's like."

"Tomorrow meet us after school and bring shorts."

"Cool."

I walk away, feeling myself. All I want is an eight boat to race at regattas, and for us to do the second race with just the Strong Four. Coach Jessica is thrilled that Pookie G. transferred over to Manley to cox.

A couple days after the race, we are feeling beat up and Coach Jessica gives us the day off to recover after the St. Louis regatta. Malcolm, Pookie G., and I decide to go to Alvin's crib to hang out and play cards. I can't find Preston. I figure he had to head home to babysit his little sister or something. We sit around Alvin's kitchen table and play spades and have *The Miseducation of Lauryn Hill* blasting in the background.

"Where y'all think Preston is getting these expensive new clothes from?" Malcolm asks. I see Alvin cut his eye at Malcolm.

"His mom, she slangs, y'all know that," I reply.

"Tell 'em, joe, tell 'em, joe," Malcolm tells Alvin. *Here we go again, Malcolm stirring up trouble,* I think to myself.

"Tell me what?" I ask.

"Preston out there working them corners after practice, I'm not gonna sugarcoat you," Malcolm says.

"But he going to practice," Alvin adds.

I feel like I just swallowed my Adam's apple, but this explains why Preston is hanging with Big Cliff all the time.

"Was this supposed to be a secret from me?"

"Ray Charles can see that, bruh," Malcolm says. Pookie G. starts laughing. That's the first we hear from him tonight. If he is going to cox, he better locate some confidence.

"Let's just finish playing," I say. I am not sure why Malcolm and Alvin swept this under the rug, but I have to talk Preston out of that life.

After Pookie G. and Malcolm leave, I sit on the porch to chill with Alvin.

"How is everything with the fam?" I ask.

"They are always in some trouble or about to fight, and I am the first they come to get for the rescue."

"Alvin, you have to let them learn, man."

"You don't get it, there are some things at home that happen to them that I let slide and I have to make up for that."

"Your dad?" I ask. Alvin's eyes get watery.

"Man, bruh, I don't discuss my dirty family laundry. I will tell you this, though. Rowing makes you forget that the world is on fire."

"The sport is changing your life, Alvin."

"Amen to that."

"What's with you and Grace?"

"Nothing really, I want her, but crew is taking over."

"That sport is changing your life," Alvin says back.

"Amen to that."

When I get home, my mom is sleeping on the couch with her Bible on her chest. I'm so proud of her. She's working at a nursing home with my aunt and is busy all the time now. Isaac and Pamela are getting tall and becoming more respectful. I think a combination of Mom having extra cash to give them what they want and attending the Victory Outreach youth service helps. We don't see Shaundell much at all but get occasional phone calls. My mom is hoping with him expecting a child soon that he will slow down with the street life.

Mom has given me the freedom to allow Ken and the rowing team to be like a second family to me. It's different for Alvin and Malcolm because their dads don't really trust white people, which I'm sure comes from personal experience.

The rowing culture at the lagoon is all about being competitive in high school, getting recruited to college, making the national rowing team, and hopefully the Olympics. While St. Ignatius and Loyola are all about what happens in the boat, our focus is more on how this unlikely lifeboat is changing our lives outside of it. Bringing rival gangs to Philly, putting them in a shell, and having black kids race in this sport has already been an enormous accomplishment. There is no more noble trophy we can gain. Today, our practice is to focus on getting the new guys up to speed on the sport and preparing the Strong Four for Iowa. We are less than a month away, and I am pissed off because a half hour has passed, and there are no sounds of Preston and Malcolm. If we win in Iowa, we can bring medals back to the school and show the other teams at the lagoon we can compete. It will be our last race of the season, then we are back to indoor racing on the erg. What we are training for is the big spring regatta in Grand Rapids, Michigan. St. Ignatius Loyola will be entering that race also. We don't care about the other teams; we want to beat them.

Ken is teaching the new kids the basics on the ergs, and Coach Jessica is giving Pookie G. the rundown when it comes to coxing. Ken is still working on finding Coach Victor's replacement. I hope it's someone black, but Ken is not going to find black coaches in rowing. If he does, I bet money they already have a job.

Coach Jessica calls for Alvin, Elliot, Josh, and me to row in a four today and Pookie G. will cox. I know she chooses Josh because of his height and athleticism. He never rowed, but he caught on fast on the erg. I just hope Josh can shut up and listen and Pookie G. doesn't row us into a wall. Ken stays on land to work with the others.

I am in stroke, Alvin is in three, Josh is in two, and Elliot is in the bow. It feels weird without Preston and Malcolm. The boat is like a spinal cord connecting us all, and if pieces are detached, it hurts.

We push off, and I can hear Josh second-guessing.

"What do I do?" he screams.

"Don't let go of your oar!" I yell back.

Coach Jessica, in her launch boat, asks for Elliot to lay his blades on the water at way enough while Alvin and I take them for a ride and row.

She gives Pookie G. some direction. I am sitting in the stroke seat, so I help him out a bit to keep the boat straight. Alvin and I take off rowing, moving in sync and showing off, going at 36 strokes per minute. Three hundred meters in, we are heading straight for the St. Ignatius boat on the opposite side of the course.

"Starboard hold water!" Coach Jessica shouts. Pookie G. has lost control of the boat and is enjoying the ride.

"You guys need help?" the coxswain from the St. Ignatius boat asks while they stroke and laugh.

"We good, homie," Alvin says.

"Y'all should've warned us that we were going drunk driving," Josh says, laughing. Everyone starts laughing, including the crew of the St. Ignatius boat. We get back at it and begin running drills. After practice, I sit with Josh and show him how to pull the launch in, and Alvin works with Dwayne on the erg. Its mind-blowing that Alvin was chasing him just a year ago.

Afterward, Coach Jessica questions me about Preston and Malcolm.

"I will check on them today, Coach."

I take the bus over to Preston's and feel nervous walking into the old neighborhood. Michelle opens the door and greets me with a big hug.

"Where you been, boy?"

"Staying out of trouble."

"That's good. Preston is in back."

I walk into Preston's room and he's ironing his clothes.

"Coop! What's up, nigga?"

"Hey, man, what happened to practice?"

"Listen, man, I'm tryna make this money."

"Me, too, that's why I'm doing this row thing."

He laughs. "Listen, Coop, you do you and I'm going to do me."

"The guys told me you're selling, man."

"They ratted me out, huh, Coop? They can't be trusted."

"Don't be stupid, we all are brothers," I say.

"Alvin's your new best friend now."

"You're my brother, and don't need the street life. How is it going to end? You saw how it ended for Derrick, Chino, Darius, and all the guys we grew up knowing. They're dead."

"Coop, Five O is onto my mom, so I have to go out here and feed my family and that six dollars an hour they giving our people is a joke."

"You should talk to Ken," I plead.

"Ken and rowing taught me more than you know, but it doesn't put food on the table and stop the kids from Manley clowning me if I don't have new threads. The streets are calling, and rowing will have to wait."

Preston pulls out a blunt and starts to roll it.

"I'm out!" I say.

"Hang out, Coop, be a friend and not a captain."

"Preston, you will get a better high off rowing, and the difference between the two is one kills brain cells, and the other leads to greatness. You know where to find me."

My attempt to talk to Preston was an epic fail. It was as if he was someone else. For some people, you have to keep an eye on them from the rearview mirror and keep moving forward. I love him, but I want to get out of the West Side and stay alive.

I get home and call Malcolm.

"Malcolm, where were you?"

"My dad took me off the team, man, and it's causing too many problems between him and my momma."

"This can't be happening."

"Honestly, Arshay, I am jealous of you all. I can't do this anymore. Rowing is all I have. I hate the work—Why would anyone want to suffer like that. But the brotherhood gave me a sense of belonging. My dad doesn't care for Jews, man, and he dislikes Ken. He doesn't like the fact that a white man is coming and trying to change black kids' lives. So, my dad said if I'm around Ken again, he will punish me, and God knows what else.

"Did Ken tell you what people are saying?"

"No," I answer.

"That Ken got us rowing out there like a bunch of kids in a slave ship?"

I'm speechless. I say I am sorry and will try to figure things out. Malcolm asks that I say nothing because he doesn't need crazy Ken knocking on his door. I feel bad losing one of the smartest guys I know. I feel like I can't do this anymore. *How can a teenage boy go through so much in four years of high school?* I knew Ken was being criticized for trying to turn us white, but he is just giving us access to something new and trying to diversify the sport. I don't know why the world is so complicated. Now I understand what Dr. Martin Luther King Jr. meant when he said, "I just want to do God's will" out of frustration.

The next day after school, I see Alvin and ask if he wants to go to Ken's office with me to catch him up on the team. He says no, and asks if I've noticed he's been limping. I haven't.

"What happened?"

"I have a hernia, and my dad said I would need surgery."

"No, man! We race Iowa soon."

He tells me he can't row, and I can't help but think about how things are falling apart. No Preston, Malcolm, and now no Alvin. He tells me he will be back before I know it, but I feel like every time we're about to fly, gravity comes and pulls us down. It seems like everything I care about goes downhill—Shaundell, Grace, winning races, now these three guys. Rowing teaches us when an unexpected crab comes your way, lay back and it let pass, don't let it knock you out of the boat but try to recover, and that is what I am going to do.

. . .

I get to Ken's office and everyone looks really busy and acts like they don't see me. There are computer screens everywhere with thousands of numbers on them. It makes me think of the movie *Trading Places* with Eddie Murphy. People are screaming and shouting curse words like crazy. I know Ken is a trader, but I don't really understand what that means.

When I see Ken, he introduces me to everyone. Most are nice and a few others are a little confused. Ken tells me he wants me to sit in on a meeting with him.

"What meeting?"

"Just a bunch of jag-offs asking for money."

"What do you mean 'asking for money'?"

He tells me they want him to invest in their project, and I tell him I will sit in.

Two white men walk in with black suits and Ken asks me to stay for the meeting. They look annoyed.

Ken informs them, "Arshay, here, is my ears, so let's hear it." I don't really understand what's going on in the meeting, but I know I want to attend more so I *can* understand.

Ken decides to drive me home. While we drive, he explains trading to me and how he thinks drug dealers would make good traders because they're leaders, take risks, and make quick decisions.

"If you play video games and are good with math, you can be a good trader."

He asks if I want to learn, but I tell him that I want to cook or work with youth.

"Cool. Did you look at any cooking schools for college?"

"Yes, I looked into Johnson & Wales, the Culinary Institute of America, the Cooking and Hospitality Institute of Chicago, and Cornell University. They have a hotel management program."

Ken looks at me. "Cornell also has rowing."

"That sounds cool."

I tell him that the cooking instructor wants me to work for free on Fridays cooking at the Hilton Chicago O'Hare Airport Hotel.

"An internship is awesome for you. Trust me, it will be a good payoff."

"Yes, but the idea of working for free is crazy. I can work and make cash."

"Work for free, trust me." I tell him okay, then I tell him about the full schedule Chef Mike Singleton has set me up with this year.

"Like what?"

"Serve at the mayor's dinner, work at the chocolate factory, and cook at the Palmer House Hilton." Ken tells me that Manley is doing a good job of getting me out there, and now I have to stay committed.

"When you're done with cooking school and college I will hook you up with a friend of mine named Rick. He's one of the owners of one of the best restaurants in Chicago. It's called Blackbird and the kitchen is run by Chef Paul Kahan." I tell him I don't know who that is, but that it sounds amazing.

Ken asks me who is in the lineup for the Iowa race. I tell him I'm thinking Pookie G. as coxswain. Ken is shocked by that because Pookie G. never talks, but I think he will.

"I will row stroke seat, and this new guy, Dwayne, will be in three seat for Alvin, because Alvin has a hernia. There's also this new kid, Josh. You'll love him. He is one of the funniest dudes I know, but you can't tell him that. He will row two seat. Elliot will be in bow."

"Where are Malcolm and Preston?"

"They said they need time away to do other stuff." I feel bad lying but I don't want be a tattle.

"What? They were so invested."

"You should call them, Ken."

"I will."

"I am going to help Coach Jessica with the team though."

Ken thanks me and tells me Coach Jessica let him know that I've been taking on a leadership role.

"Yeah, I've been reading this book on leadership by John C. Maxwell that's been helping me. I feel like we need more of a direction."

Ken asks where I got the book, and I tell him that a guy at church gave me twenty bucks to read it.

"That's awesome. I'll find a new coach to kick your butts." I thank him, and tell him he should come to church with me sometime.

"Maybe not."

"Why?"

"I don't have a problem with Jesus. I just have a problem with his people." I tell him I've never heard that before and we both laugh.

A few weeks have passed and Josh, Elliot, Malcolm, Dwayne, Pookie G., and I have been grinding at the boathouse. They're not as strong as Preston, Malcolm, and Alvin but they are very technical and got cardio for days. We will do a two-hour practice session and afterward play basketball for another two hours at the court. Spending time at the boathouse has become our thing. We hang out with Eugene, kayak, fix boats, and just chill and watch the master's team scull. School can be chaotic on a daily basis, so the boathouse is where we go to download serenity. Alvin is healing and can't wait to get back at it. Malcolm swings by Alvin's place occasionally but still can't come to the boathouse. Preston stopped coming to school, and that blows.

I think the team is ready for Iowa. We are racing in a head race. This means boats begin with a moving start at periods of ten to twenty seconds and it's all about time. The cool thing is sometimes you can't tell who is first or last until it's posted because boats are flying past one by one. While juniors typically race 1,500 meters, this race is 4,000 meters, which means we finish or die trying. We are racing against many teams from the Midwest. For a team that was put together in less than a month, we are the underdogs with big hearts. America loves the underdog story. What I can't wrap my head around is how we glorify the underdog to the top and when they make it and continue to win, we get tired of seeing them there and hope to see them fall to the next underdog.

The night is here. I find myself in the corn fields of Iowa, surrounded by nothing familiar. This state has horror-movie potential. It's dark, and the cabins we drive past are creepy; now I am just waiting to see a scarecrow.

I feel confident in the guys I am racing with, although it is weird rowing without Preston, Malcolm, and Alvin. Teammates seldom have any clue about the effect it has on you when they quit a team, get suspended, or get injured. Everything becomes heavier.

It is a quiet ride to the lake in Coach Jessica's truck. Josh is growing on us and keeps us laughing, but he never says much about his personal life. When I bring up family, he changes the subject.

Dwayne has caught on to rowing pretty quickly, and tells me that it's by far the hardest sport he's done in his life. Pookie G. has been talking a little more, and spends a lot of time with me and Alvin while he's recovering. He is super smart and has a lovely mother who believes I will be rich one day. Every time she sees me she asks when I'm going to buy her a house.

Elliot is pumped and still working at the Marriott since Ken got him the job. He is just so humble and does whatever he is told. He tells us that this team changed his life. He says crew keeps him sane.

As we pull up to the race, Josh asks where our boat is and Coach Jessica tells us we will share someone else's boat. The beautiful thing about crew culture is that they share equipment with each other. Josh asks if they know we're black and Coach Jessica laughs.

"We will see."

"And not Carlton black," Josh says, "Wesley Snipes black."

We crack up.

"Okay, guys," Coach Jessica tells us, "I'm going to check on equipment so just hang out and stay close."

Josh jumps out of the car and starts scoping out all the ladies with pink toes, and I tell him to keep it cool. He tells me I need to chill and enjoy being a teenager, but it's race time.

"Dude," Josh says to me, "before we race, we should come out like the Chicago Bulls. We can bebop the theme song. *'From North Lawndale, rowing in stroke seat, Arshay Cooperrrrr.'*"

I start laughing and tell him it's not a bad idea. It is a different vibe than the other races. At most races, people just stare at us, but at this one it seems like they don't want us there. The staff isn't as nice to us as they were at previous races, so we stay to ourselves. Pookie G. senses it, too, and tells me to look at Josh. I look over and Josh is throwing pennies into the crowd, but they can't see where they're coming from because of the size of the crowd. I walk toward Josh to tell him to stop.

"It's those damn black guys," someone screams.

Josh balls up a fist. "You hear what they just said about us?"

"Dude," I tell him, "it *is* those damn black guys. Chill the hell out, man." We walk off without looking back.

I see Coach Jessica walking toward us urgently and I think we're in trouble.

"Guys, our race is starting now. There was some miscommunication. You have to row 2,000 meters out of the start and you may not have time to rest."

I ask her if we have to sprint to the start.

"Yes, because you guys are starting late."

I'm not happy about that, but we get the boat, walk it to the dock, and quickly jump in. We start rowing to the start line, saying every curse word in the book.

"You think they're cheating us?" Josh asks.

"Maybe," Elliot says, but I just row. I angrily tell Pookie G. that he has to motivate us and give us something.

"Row," he says lightly. I give up on him and try to motivate them myself, but the boat is not well balanced.

"Port, raise your oar, and starboard, lower yours!" I scream, and the boat balances.

Boats are flying off the start line as we pull up; the staff in the motorboat tells us we need to quickly turn and go because all seven of the boats are already gone.

"We just got here, can we get a break?" I ask, but they tell me no, we need to turn now and row. It is brutal. My hands are starting to bleed, my back is hurting, and I know it is going to be all heart. We are driving back with all our strength and I feel the boat moving. The race is so long and we don't see anyone in sight. Out of nowhere, Pookie G. starts screaming.

"Okay, fools, let's do this." We are all in shock.

"Power ten strokes in two," he screams. "One, two, now!"

He counts down with each stroke and is shouting at us, telling us we got this. He is saying anything that comes to mind and cursing like crazy. It's funny, but at the same time it is working.

We finally pass the finish line, feeling half-past dead. We lean back on each other's laps. When we get off the boat, Coach Jessica is smiling.

"You boys just became men."

We can't say a word, we are so tired.

"You guys basically sprinted over four miles straight, that's impressive. You raced all college teams from Iowa and came in last by two seconds, and that's only because of that 2,000 meter pre-race sprint that shouldn't have happened. I'm sorry about that. I believe you could have placed first."

Coach Jessica heads off to wrap things up and we're in the parking lot laughing and repeating some of the stuff Pookie G. was saying. And that, in and of itself, is one helluva story.

13

2K

Winter in Chicago feels like a pair of windshield wipers, slapping you from side to side for four months straight. It's December, so I know it's just beginning, but I already see people walking backward in the street because the wind is so strong it stings their faces. Some tall buildings have large, sharp icicles hanging off the roofs, so the city blocks off a lot of the sidewalks. Public transportation is overcrowded because so many cars have frozen gas tanks. I see neighbors arguing in the street over a bucket they use to hold their parking spot to prevent someone else from taking it. We get so much snow that it can take hours to shovel out a parking spot, only to have a neighbor steal it from you the minute it's clear. Up and down the streets of the city, there are buckets, chairs, and traffic cones "saving" freshly shoveled parking spots for people when they leave for work. Some people respect the saved spots, but when someone doesn't, there is almost always a fight.

In spite of the freezing cold, I've learned to find beauty in the city. I've been on Christmas break for the last few days, so I'm using the money I've saved to explore. In my sixteen years of living I have never had a teacher, family member, or friend tell me to go and get lost in the city I was born and raised in. I have dreams of traveling and exploring other cities and countries, but how can I if I've never seen the four corners of my own?

I fall in love walking down State Street, it is so beautiful. Christmas music is playing in front of Marshall Field's and people look so happy coming in and out of the building. Even the street preacher in front of Old Navy looks happy telling everyone that they are condemned to hell. I walk past Daley Plaza and there is a huge Christmas tree with people singing in front; pictures are being taken of Baby Jesus and the angels. I walk into the Borders bookstore and have never seen so many books in my life. I'm amazed at the number of young people that are there sitting on the floor, just to read. Across the street from Borders is the Chicago Theatre. I am too scared to walk inside; it looks so fancy, so I just stare through the window. I walk over to Michigan Avenue and it's filled with people carrying shopping bags. I stare up at the Wrigley Building, which reminds me of Gotham City. It looks like an old castle, unbreakable. I stick around and admire the Chicago street talent, the kids beating buckets with their drumsticks, the saxophone players, and the singers out in the cold hustling for change. I take a bus to Hyde Park and check out the huge houses that leave me in awe. I also find beauty in the inner city of Chicago, like the talented old men on Madison Street who sing in front of garbage cans full of burning wood to keep warm. They sound flawless. I admire the kids on the West Side who shovel snow off the outdoor basketball court to play ball. Even the cold can't keep them from being dedicated to their sport.

The Christmas lights on South Homan Avenue and West Flournoy Street are amazing. What the community does with that block during the holidays is better than any Christmas decorations I've seen on TV. Mad Christmas lights of all colors connect every apartment building and lamppost on the block. It's basically a mini Macy's on the West Side.

It's nice to see churches get together and give cheerfully to the homeless, and see community centers put on creative holiday events. The brotherhood at barbershops and the positive image they give young kids is never talked about, but those guys deserve an award, especially my barber Dee.

I have a reality check, because my head is so filled with negativity from what the media shows me and what I hear on the radio about gangs, drug dealers, the corrupt politicians, crooked cops, city segregation, and poor public schools. I know these things shouldn't be ignored, but I'm ready to hear about solutions and not just the problems. At one time I believed that there was no good left in Chicago, and this exploration reminds me of all of its beauty, culture, and goodness.

My mom and I finish unwrapping some Christmas gifts and I think back to the times when we didn't have Christmas. To see us now is amazing. My mom is always dancing around because she's been seeing one of the leaders from the church. His name is Keith Pearson and he's a great musician. He is the same guy who pays kids to read books. Now that I think about it, I am probably the only kid he's paid. My whole family is here celebrating and jamming to the *Jackson Five Christmas Album*. Grandma is in the kitchen, cooking up some soul food with my aunts and uncle. Shaundell is playing a Sonic game with Isaac, and he had a beautiful baby boy. There is not a single drug addict in my family anymore. My mom's faith has saved us all. The Cooper family has beaten the odds, and we all feel it's our responsibility to give hope to every person or group we encounter. The excellent news is Shaundell decided that he is going into the Victory Outreach men's home in Rockford, Illinois, to separate himself from the gangs.

I tell my mom I will see her later and head to Ken's for an early Christmas dinner. When I get to their place, Jeni is playing the Puff Daddy & the Family album. I tell her she never seems to let me down when it comes to music and she laughs. They're both preparing dinner so I decide to go out and help their neighbor shovel snow. Her name is Olga and she is a tall white woman with short white hair. She's also the head surgeon for Cook County Hospital. I always have cool conversations with her about food. We get along very well. The first few times we spoke, it was basically her telling the boys and I to keep it down when we were too loud in the backyard.

"You have amazing abilities," Jeni says. "Our friends like you more than they like us."

I find myself hanging with Ken and his friends Bob Muzikowski, Marty Murray, and Russ Greenberg a lot. I sit, listen, and learn every time I'm around those guys. Russ manages Ken's real estate business and he calls the rowing team anytime he needs help with simple labor so we can make extra cash.

As we sit down for dinner, Ken tells me we have a new coach named Marc Mandel.

"That's cool. I hope he can handle everyone."

"He will be great, make it easy for him."

Jeni has set out a beautiful dinner, and we eat until we can't eat any more. The food is to die for, and afterward we open gifts. I know I can't give Ken and Jeni something they don't already have, so I write them a beautiful card and give them chocolates. Jeni gives me a book to read called *The Four Agreements*. I open the cover and quickly read over the main points and I am instantly hooked. I open another gift and it is a small gold chain that I admired at the mall once when Ken and I went to get clothes for Winnifred. I choke up a bit and tell them I can't thank them enough. I wonder, *Who am I that life is so wonderful to me?* Life used to be so bad for me that jumping off a bridge was a daydream. People like to say life gets better, but to me it isn't just a saying. It is the truth.

I sit at the table, deep in my thoughts like Kevin from *The Wonder Years*, not hearing the words that are coming out of Ken's and Jeni's mouths. Everything fades away and I think about how Jeni is just like an apple. If you can get past the tough skin, you will see her sweetness. I see the star she really is and will become. I think about Ken, too. From the moment I first met him, Ken has exposed me to higher education, Ivy League colleges, healthy living, traveling, finding my purpose, and understanding the needs of the world. He has never given up on us and has been faithful and positive every step of the way. I am grateful for my internship at the Hilton Chicago O'Hare Airport Hotel, the rowing team, and the entrepreneurship classes. I have accomplished more in two years than I had in the fourteen years before.

I'm back at school after Christmas break and it's amazing catching up with my teammates. Alvin got a new job working at a shoe store in the North Riverside Park Mall and he tells me to come to his job for a hookup on shoes. He also tells me he has a new car and I can't wait to see it.

A couple of weeks ago, Alvin and I ate at IHOP and he somehow got the phone number of a Mexican girl named Maria who doesn't speak any English. He is still seeing her, and I ask how they communicate.

"We point."

I laugh. "I don't even want to know what that means."

He tells me he's always wanted a girl that doesn't talk his ear off.

Josh is busy being a teenager, making people laugh. He has dreams of going to The Second City and hiring me as his booking agent. Josh brags about not being a video game crackhead anymore. He says writing jokes takes up all his time now. Elliot is working part time as a cook at the Marriott Hotel. Pookie G. is talking a lot more and has been spending time at home. He is such a homebody. His mom is dating a guy who looks like he's fresh out of the joint. Every time we go to Pookie G.'s place, the guy is sweeping the floor and there is never any dirt. He only ever gives us head nods and says, "What up, li'l niggas?"

After Iowa, we went right into the indoor season. I can't wait for the weather to break and to get back on the water. Our weeks have been all about conditioning, erging, homework help, and learning from each other. Coach Jessica has held it down alone from fall into early winter.

We're all really excited to meet the new coach, so I meet Alvin after class and we walk down to the gym room together. Alvin tells me about his idea to start a moving company.

"Dude, you have money?"

"I will ask Ken, since he teaches entrepreneurship."

We walk into the gym room and see the new coach. Marc Mandel is a skinny guy with pale skin and freckles. He has curly red hair that matches the red rings around his eyes. He looks like he's never slept. He has a friendly face and I feel like he may not last a single day in this school. Ken and Jessica bring us all in.

"Okay, guys, listen up! Get dressed, and I will introduce you to the new coach and we'll start practice," Ken says.

In the men's locker room, Josh says, "What the hell? Our new coach is the male Punky Brewster."

"I know, man," I tell him. "I have to talk to Ken about this."

"You better, because I will clown this guy all year."

Alvin tells Josh to calm down and we get dressed and walk back upstairs.

Ken introduces us to Marc and asks if he'd like to say a few words.

Marc stands up. "Hey, guys, I'm happy to be here and I promise you if you do what I ask, I will make you guys fast."

"We will do everything but wear that damn spandex," Josh tells him, "because we are *blessed* and can't have people staring."

We start laughing.

"Yeah, man, we can't wear that."

Marc grins and starts looking at our hands. "You can tell a dedicated rower by their hands. The more calluses you have, the harder you work. You guys can use some more blisters.

"Hey, guys, my name is Marc Mandel. I rowed at Northwestern University and just graduated this year."

"This is your first coaching job?" Josh asks.

"This is. I am excited to be the men's coach, and Coach Jessica will focus on building a girls' team here at Manley."

"So, you won't be coaching us?" I ask Jessica.

"I will be around, don't worry," she replies.

Marc continues, "We are in the winter, so the focus is to get you guys racing 2,000 meters against other junior rowers in the city. College coaches look at your erg scores, SAT scores, and GPA. I am here to bring those up and get you into a school if you want to row in college. This requires a commitment on my end and yours. After the winter season, we go back to Philly for spring break camp, we scrimmage and race in Grand Rapids at the high school invitational regatta and bring home those medals to Manley and our family.

"Okay, sixty laps around the gym," he says, starting to run. We quietly mumble complaints about having to do sixty laps. Ken runs with us as well, and he, Marc, Pookie G., and I am in front the whole time. The gym isn't that big, so sixty laps is really only two miles but after thirty laps we are all slowing down.

"I'm sure you guys are faster than this!" Marc screams. "Come on, guys, push it!"

Marc is in top shape, and while we're running, he tells us he wouldn't ask us to do something that can't be done, so he will always be right there doing it with us. Marc slows down and gets behind me.

"You're the captain . . . let's get at it!"

He keeps running a few paces behind me so there is no room for me to slack. I push myself until every last lap is completed. I can't breathe. I squat down but Marc tells me to stand up, it's good for me. While the other guys are finishing up he asks me to help him set up the erg machines. I'm really dying, and showing it.

Marc tells me, "We get tired but don't show it—it's a sign of weakness."

All the other guys finish and start walking toward the door. Marc stops them.

"Hold up, no water right now. We're not finished warming up." Some of the guys begin complaining but I tell them we're not done yet.

Alvin throws his hands up. "Oookay, let's get it over with." We sit on the rowing machines and Marc walks over and sets the timer for forty minutes.

"Oh, hell naw!" Josh yells. There is a mixture of laughing and coughing because we are so tired.

Marc gives us all a smirk. "Oh, hell yes. Okay, let's go, arms only."

We row arms only until they go numb, then add arms and body, and then full body. He critiques every movement we make. I feel like it is my first day rowing, as if I'm not doing anything right. Marc is a technical man and during every drive I take on the erg, he is staring at my feet, hands, face, and back. It is hard for me to concentrate. Alvin lets go of the handle.

"This is crazy!"

We've all been waiting for the first person to say it. Marc tells us all to pause. He steps over to Alvin and passes the handle back to him.

"You never let go of this oar. You just gave up on every person in the boat. You want to do that to yourself, fine, but don't forget you're not in that boat alone. We are all one in that boat."

Alvin grabs the handle with his head down.

"When you are in that boat, people are going to watch you more than they watch themselves. You guys are super strong, and I'm going to give you the tools to win a race. Back to catch and row."

I look at Marc and I know he is the nightmare that I asked for who will push me past my limits, until I know that I am fully awake and always ready to go.

After practice, Marc talks to us one by one and explains our strengths and weaknesses. He tells us that there is a Chicago indoor racing championship in a few weeks that we will be racing in.

"It's a 2,000-meter piece. I am going to test you all tomorrow and I will prepare you for it." I nod. "Good job today, guys."

I think about what he said. A 2,000-meter piece on the erg is painful. I tested myself in the summer and I rowed 2,000 meters in 7 minutes and 31 seconds. I want to beat that time. When I walk into the locker room, all the guys are complaining again. I tell them what I think: Marc is great, a welcome change.

"I know," Alvin says, "but to start off that way is insane."

The other guys agree.

Pookie G. isn't happy either. "I cox the boat and still have to do it!"

Josh tells me he thinks Marc is a redheaded monster. I agree, but I know he is going to make us faster so I'm willing to wait it out.

When we get to Alvin's apartment, his big brother is there. I've never met him, and Alvin has only spoken of him a few times. Alvin tells me he is a dealer on the South Side who buys a new car every month. He looks as scary as Alvin's dad, about six-two and 300 pounds. He's dark and bald with bloodshot eyes and scarred knuckles. He shouts to Alvin and tells him to come into the other room; it seems urgent, so I hang back. I wonder what's going on. Alvin comes back and tells me he has to go.

"What's up, man?"

"Something went down, and I have to help my brother."

I shake my head and say, "Don't do it." Alvin tears up, and he turns around and leaves. I watch them get in his brother's car and drive off. His brother never looks at me once.

I think about what Alvin said on the bus in Philly. He said he'd only ever been in a fight to protect his family and friends. He said his dad told him he would end up in jail or dead protecting loved ones. It is exactly what has me worried.

I head home and chill, hoping that Alvin will call and tell me what happened. I pray Alvin will be smart. He is highly intelligent. He's won chess competitions, he can hear a song three times and remember every word, he can solve any problem he learns in class, and he's a good reader. To me, smart is more than just understanding puzzles, remembering words, or quoting facts. To me, intelligence is being able to stay out of trouble, knowing when to shut your mouth, being open to new learning, hanging out with the right crowd, and thinking of consequences before every action. I know Alvin has changed, and now I'm worried.

He calls a few hours later and doesn't sound good.

"What's wrong? What happened?"

"Man, I feel so bad. The guy my brother is working with messed up his money, and he wanted me to help jump him. Man, that's not me anymore."

"So, what happened?"

"My brother went to his house and rang the doorbell, and the guy came out talking crazy. I ran up and started hitting him with a pool stick."

"God, Alvin."

"What do I do? It's my brother. I don't feel right. How am I going to hit someone with a pool stick, then go to church with you on the weekend?"

"Listen, there was a time when you would beat someone up, and you didn't care or feel bad. Now you do. You *are* changing, man. This life isn't for you anymore."

I tell him he has to come to church with me, and he says he will on Sunday. We hang up the phone, and my heart is heavy for him. At the same time, I'm angry. I'm mad about where we live and how we're growing up. I'm pissed that the odds are always stacked against us, so everything is a struggle. I'm jealous of the guys we race because the odds are with them. I wonder if it makes rowing—and life—easier for them.

After class, I walk Grace to the bus stop quickly, because Marc is a no-nonsense coach who doesn't condone tardiness.

"Arshay, I want to express my gratitude to you because you stuck by my side and always take the time to walk me to the bus stop." It sounds like she is ready to give me a shot.

"Hey, that's what I do, but we have a new coach, and I have to run to practice. Tomorrow's walk's on me. So, please hold that thought."

"Well, you go, boy."

I sprint back to the school.

I change in the locker room and then run up to the gym where Marc and the guys are already running. I join the line and Marc informs us we have to do ten more laps. "No being late." They all look at me, pissed off, and Alvin shakes his head. I guess, in a way, I'm hardheaded. I just don't like giving up on people or things unless they're hurting me. I'm not sure if wanting to be with Grace is hurting me.

After the run, Marc has us take out the ergs and set us up to test for a 2K. That is 2,000 meters. When you meet someone who rows, they usually ask you what's your 2K. That's how rowers size each other up. In practice is Josh, Alvin, Elliot, Pookie G., and myself. Dwayne never came back after the Iowa race. He said crew is tougher than tough and takes up too much of a teenager's life. This pain and sport are only for the tenacious. We all grab our oars and take off. I sprint my first six strokes then ease right into it. My goal is to finish in 7 minutes and 15 seconds. I know coaches look for a 6:20 for men, but that's not happening. Everyone in the room is screaming and pulling. The key is to relax and push. Marc is walking around giving pointers. I am halfway through, and this hurts like hell. Every time I sit on this machine I ask myself why I am doing this. Indoor season is all a mental game and it's hard not to let doubt creep in. I should have my tunes. I feel the team slowing down. I try to gather my second wind, but my batteries are low. I finish in 7 minutes and 29 seconds. I fall onto the floor with my feet still in the foot stretcher, too tired to unstrap it, and Marc yells, "No, sit up!" I finished first in the group. Then Alvin, Elliot, and Josh. Pookie G. is still going, so we all rally around to motivate him by shouting and clapping. Coxswains don't usually do 2Ks, but Pookie G. did. We have to carry him out of the gym.

"You guys did very well. Just a few announcements. Arshay will compete in the indoor competition, everyone else has to bring their score down a bit more. Here are some permission slips for spring break. I repeat, we are going to Philly again and it's going to be a hard training camp. Also, they are building a new rowing site on the South Side and you guys will help to be a part of that project.

"This is going to be a great year, and if you guys keep showing up, I will take you to the famous Buffalo Joe's and visit my college, Northwestern University."

I ask him what Buffalo Joe's is.

"The best wings spot in the world." Josh asks if they have watermelon in a very sarcastic tone and we start laughing again. Marc doesn't crack a single smile.

We spend the next two weeks running and doing the erg machine nonstop. I am in prime shape and run everywhere. Everyone in school is noticing our transformation. Marc is the right man for the job; he is a lion in sheep's clothing. His appearance seems so fragile but his roar is strong.

On Saturday, Marc picks me up for the Chicago Indoor Rowing competition and nerves are running high. My last time for 2,000 meters was 7 minutes and 29 seconds. I'm hoping to beat it by at least ten seconds. When we arrive, there are hundreds of people in the gymnasium. There are at least thirty ergs lined up at center court and chairs behind them for coaches. In front of every erg is a puke bucket. Once again, I am the only brown face in the crowd. I do see a few of the guys from Loyola St.

Ignatius, and my blood instantly raises. I am set to race in the eighteen-and-under age group. I notice there are college kids that are eighteen years old in my section, so I get a little nervous. Marc tells me that no one here is in my league.

"You're stronger than any kid I've seen on the erg machine. Remember, you have a right to be here and a right to win. I have high hopes for you, Arshay." That is all I need to hear, and I am ready. The power of speaking the right words to a young person can do something magical. I feel unstoppable.

I sit next to the stroke seat from St. Ignatius. I look at him, and he glares at me with that infamous smirk. I can't wait to race them again. I know, to them, we are just the kids who ran into the brick wall.

I sit on the erg machine, and Marc is right there next to me to coach me. He is more intense than I am. I can see the press from *Rowing News* behind me in the mirror.

"To the catch. Ready. *Row!*"

I drive back with all the strength I can gather from my legs. The wheeze of the fans from the erg machine fills the room. People are getting busy.

My arms are giving out. Marc has to push me through the last couple of minutes, yelling, "It's the heart and mind from here. You will be the champion!" I close my eyes and max out when there are 100 meters left.

"Stop!" Marc yells. "Look around you; everyone is still rowing."

I won first place! And I am so tired I can't get off the machine. I hit my goal at 7 minutes and 15 seconds. I earn a medal, and the journalist from *Rowing News* tells me they will send me a certificate that reads *Arshay Cooper, First Place* and the names of the guys I competed against. I am happy to have more material for the wall. I have become a fan of the awards that come with a strong work ethic.

"Arshay, you are good enough for me to enter you in the national indoor championship."

"Seriously, Marc?"

"Yes, I will enter you." I throw myself on the floor like a star angel and say, "I came a mighty long way."

Afterward, I ask Marc to drop me off at Ken's place, where I am going to meet Alvin. I can't wait to share the good news.

As we're driving, he says he has to talk with me about something. It sounds serious.

"I have been questioning your leadership because you've been late to all of our practices. It's not fair for the guys to do extra work because you're walking a girl to the bus stop. Meet her after. I'm down for love, but you have a responsibility to your guys. Alvin stepped up to tell me the truth about how much this person means to you."

In my head, I'm thinking that everyone deserves that high school sweetheart, but quickly I realize I'm not anyone's sweetheart. Grace is my friend, but the person that makes me smile is also the same person that makes me frown. I realize Marc is teaching me about discipline but I have a feeling he knows more and wants me to get over her and stay focused.

"I got a taste of what I can do today," I tell Marc, "and whatever I have to do to see more success, I'm going to do it."

When I get to the house, Alvin is there playing Ken in chess.

I go in to chill with Jeni for a little bit and talk new music. After hanging with Ken and Jeni for a couple hours, they decide to take us home. They first drop Alvin off near his place. We drive south on Kedzie and, as we turn onto Harrison, I hear the tires of a car making a sharp turn. Behind us now is a black Crown Victoria police car; I see the cops inside looking directly at me. I tell Jeni we're about to get pulled over, but Ken tells me to relax.

They hit the sirens.

"See, you not only get pulled over for driving while black but being in a car while black."

The police jump out and head to the front of the Mercedes. As soon as they realize who is in the front seats, you can see the look of surprise on their faces. I'm sure we got pulled over because only drug dealers in Alvin's neighborhood drive Mercedes. The officer approaches the driver's side and Jeni rolls the window down.

"What's the problem?"

"You rolled a left turn in front of me. You should have slowed down."

"That's BS; you were a block away. It's obvious why you pulled us over."

The cop is seething. He tells Ken he should calm her down before he locks her up.

"Calm down, Jeni."

"No, Ken. You saw that they were a block away." Jeni turns back to the cop. "You gonna give me a ticket? Do it now and don't waste my time."

The cop backs up. "Next time, drive carefully."

He tells Jeni she can leave, and by the look on his face he realizes he went too far. I don't think that cop had any idea he was running into the wrong white people.

It's a quiet ride back to their house, and I start thinking about the differences and similarities between Ken and Jeni. I know Ken was raised in New Jersey with two siblings; his mother is a teacher and his dad an orthodontist. Ken went to an Ivy League college and majored in science and economics. He was a great rower and quick thinker. He moved to Chicago and made his first million in his twenties. He's a born entrepreneur and always had a heart to make a difference in the inner city. Jeni was born in Indiana with two siblings; her mother was a nurse and her dad a doctor. Her parents are divorced. Jeni went to school for music, sang opera, and was the runner-up for Miss Indiana. She realized there was a need for criminal defense attorneys and decided to go to law school.

Ken and Jeni met at a bar and hit it off, had Winnifred, and got married. I don't think they are a "single soul dwelling in two bodies" or have the chemistry of Cliff and Clair Huxtable, but they see the world the same way. They both embody the importance of working hard to have wealth, good health, friendship, family, love, and having more than enough to give. Alvin told me he thinks they both decided to get wealthy just so they had more to give. I admire their choice to live a selfless life because I've grown up around takers all my life. I think my sister's first word was "mine." Being around Ken, Jeni, and my post-Victory Outreach mom, I feel surrounded by givers and it's making my heart change. I'm torn between wanting to be a chef and wanting to help others.

It's midnight and I can't sleep. I have decided to tell Grace that she has to give "us" a shot, or I am going to move on and explore other options. This friend-zone madness has taken its toll on me. I can't sleep because I am starting to come to my senses and realize that if she wanted to be with me it would have happened already. It's been awhile since I asked her about our relationship so I am still holding on to an ounce of faith that she will say we should go for it. I decide to force myself to sleep, because this is so confusing and love sucks.

Before practice, I tell Alvin to let Marc know that I will be a few minutes late because I have to talk to Grace.

"Dude, we'll have to run."

"No, he will understand." Alvin wishes me good luck. I walk her to the bus stop and while she is talking I am rehearsing what I am going to say to her. My heart is pounding and my legs are giving out.

"I think this is probably the last time I will say this, but I like you. What do you want to do about us?" She stops and looks at me. "Girl, I like you a lot."

"I know, and I like you a lot."

"Well, that's progress."

She stops me. "But I can't give you what you deserve."

I feel like a stupid little boy.

"You know I will need some time before I feel comfortable being just your friend," I tell her.

"Yes. And, Arshay . . . I have always been honest with you."

"I know. I just haven't been honest with myself."

I don't know if Marc, Alvin, Josh, or anyone else has ever felt what I am feeling right now. It is the worst feeling, like my chest is cut open with a knife and a blowtorch is blowing away at it. Getting punched in the face would feel better than this, and for the first time ever there is no one around to do it. I tell her I have to go, and she understands. If it were raining I would look up at the sky and cry so no one would know the difference.

I walk into the gym upset, ruined, fully clothed, and short of breath. I sit on the erg machine and just go at it. No one says a word to me or stares. They allow me to deal with what I'm going through. My thoughts are racing as I am rowing. She doesn't know that I've trained so hard to transform my body to look good for her. She doesn't know that I run extra laps, hurt my teammates, rent romantic movies, spend hours daydreaming, draw pictures, skip homework, lose sleep, and pray for her. She will never know. I tell myself that this is part of the high school experience. What is high school without a broken heart? I feel soft, like I'm not being a man. I have never seen any of my friends like this. I've also never seen them in love. I repeatedly tell myself that this is not a door closing but another door opening. I sit on the erg machine, torn apart, not because I let her go, but because it is the right thing to do.

After my workout, Alvin approaches. "I need to holla at you."

"I know, we have to finish the history project by the end of the week."

"Yeah, that, too, but Preston's boy got into an argument with S.O.A. and they're going to stomp this dude tomorrow after school. Preston will probably try to help."

"Damn, man. Preston can't do that, these guys are nuts. Can you say anything to squash it?"

"Naw, man, I tried."

"I will call Preston as soon as I get home."

He nods before asking, "You cool?"

"Yeah, man, for sure."

I haven't talked to Preston in a while. He comes to school every now and then and he is deep into the street life now. He is still my boy but we are growing separately.

When I call Preston, he tells me that if S.O.A. jumps his boy he will have to help.

"Preston, there are eighty of them and five of you."

"I don't care, and if you're not going to help me, it's all good."

I want to scream at him. Preston is so different now. I tell Preston to tell his boy to be cool, and maybe nothing will happen. I call Alvin and tell him that I don't care what the beef is, but we have the power to fix it. It's our responsibility.

"I don't ask for much, but I'm asking you to fix it."

"Alright, I get you."

I hang up, knowing he will. He has a lot of influence over those guys. Even though he doesn't roll with them anymore, they won't forget the times he's had their back. I go to bed listening to *The Quiet Storm* on the radio to make my night a little easier.

The school day goes smooth; Alvin fixed the situation between Preston's friend and S.O.A. I see Grace in the hallway and we walk right past each other. My body goes numb for a second and then I'm fine. I take a deep breath and remind myself that it's for the best.

Sweaty backs, chiseled calves, and shredded arms are what I see from the guys as I run behind them up the school stairs. Marc has been with us for over a month, and we have never been so in shape. After the next Philly camp, there is no doubt that we will be the fastest crew around. I have become obsessed with the sport, and at times I work myself sick on the erg machine. I am all about that 2K life. I wake up at sunrise, thank God, hop on the train, pick up Alvin, and we go for a run before the gangsters come out. I shower at his place, go to school and then back to training with the guys and Marc. Being in the boat with Preston, Malcolm, and Alvin was all about family, social impact, and making the impossible believable. This team I'm on with Alvin, Josh, Elliot, Pookie G. is about crossing finish lines at regattas and in life. We went from loving the sound of the basketball net to daydreaming about the echoes of the oarlocks. When you decide to row, your favorite thing becomes secondary. And that, the team considers a badge of honor.

On Wednesday is study hall. Marc is running late, and we are working on our homework. I usually have to sit with Josh to make sure he finishes his work. He has the best shot of getting recruited into college to row. He is younger and has time to get a 6:20 2K and super tall. Marc describes him as the most athletic person on the team. I know comedy is his dream, but damn, I would love to see him in the Olympics. We've only had two African American rowers in the Olympics so far—Anita DeFrantz and Patricia Spratlen. Two powerful women. I hope to shake their hands one day. I spend my spare time researching the sport, and Marc has helped break things down for me. My favorite story is when the Americans took gold in Germany.

From the classroom, we can see a bunch of guys running, and we all run to the window.

"You know the S.O.A. gang at war with the football team," Josh says to Alvin.

"I know, man," Alvin responds.

"Are you going to help? Josh asks.

"He's not," I answer.

"I can speak for myself, Arshay."

We all sit back down. "Alvin, I hope you don't help," Josh says.

"Yeah, the football team are all huge dudes, and they got animal names like Monkey Blood, Worm, Beast Tray, and Tiger," Elliot adds.

"I know, I hope S.O.A. don't use weapons," I say.

"Chumps use guns!" Josh yells.

"Listen, man; that life is over for me," Alvin says.

"Being a black man in America is the scariest thing ever," Pookie G. adds.

"Yeah. The first time I saw a dead body from violence, I was ten," Josh says.

"Nine!" Pookie G. shouts.

"Around the same time for me," Alvin says.

"I even saw my mom when she was murdered. I was a baby," Elliot says, staring out the window.

I remember Elliot telling me that one time in the gym room.

"Sorry, bruh, my mom's not around," Josh adds.

"I don't live with my mom," Alvin says.

"My father is nowhere in sight," I say.

"I second that," Pookie G. murmurs.

"But now I am worried about Malcolm," Pookie adds.

"He has been wearing new threads from head to toe," Alvin says.

"He selling?" I ask.

"Maybe," Pookie says, nodding.

"Guys, can we talk about the Michigan race. This conversation is making my stomach turn," Elliot says.

We get back to work. I am puzzled. I feel bad for Preston and especially Malcolm. I do not want to lose them for threads. If you pull a kid out of an afterschool program or kick them out, there is a risk of them doing all kinds of wrong. I would like to say the violence in Chicago is decreasing, but it's not. People are dirt poor out here, barely surviving, and it doesn't help that they can locate a gun. What the white guys on TV with their fancy suits don't understand is that for at least some, if you get them a good-paying job, you can keep them from breaking into your house. I can't explain why folks from the hood resort to using guns. It used to be they would be break dancing to solve problems. I know as a kid, all the local stores sold the same cheap toys.

There were cap guns to play cowboys and Indians, fake machine guns that made loud noises, and rubber knives to play cops and robbers. There were water guns to play war and shoot at strangers, or to shoot at each other to keep us cool during the summer. When the streetlights came on, it was time to go inside, so we played with our stiff green army men and lined them up to shoot at each other. We had cheap toy wrestlers and cartoon heroes to fight each other until we fell asleep. If you were lucky, you had a Nintendo. It came with a gray and black gun that everyone wanted, and we felt tough when we held it and shot at the screen. Before you knew it, guns and fighting were considered cool and the violent movies we watched just added to it. By ten years old, everyone knew how to construct make-believe paper pistols. When we got older and the real thing became easy to find, they felt familiar in our grip. On my block, you were respected for carrying a gun and criticized for carrying a book. I always hoped it would change because I didn't want other kids to grow up like I did, never knowing what it's like to feel safe.

This indoor season has been good to me so far. We are at another indoor rowing event; this time it's hosted by USRowing, a national governing body for the sport of rowing in the United States. I am in a good mode because I won a leadership trophy at the Manley Athletic Awards ceremony. I also won the award for the Best Culinary Junior at Manley. If I win this rowing event, I can be nationally ranked. The event is held at a super-cool gymnasium in the city. Rowers are racing in this event in their states all over the country. Marc entered Alvin and me in the competition. Josh, Elliot, and Pookie G. came to support.

"I got money on my boys," Josh is screaming to people sizing them up. Alvin pimp walks to his erg, looking like a rowing gangster. We are in the event for eighteen year-olds and under and we are again the only blacks in the room.

We sit on the machines to practice until it's time. There are, like, thirty other people on the ergs.

It is time, and we all take off. You can hear the flywheel on the erg playing music to our stroke. The competitive energy in the room becomes contagious for everyone. I hear Pookie G. swearing at me. "Get that shit, homie!" he yells. It doesn't sound suitable standing next to the white coxswain shouting, "Let's go, Riley!" You would think we are competing in two different places. Having my boys here is giving me the coal I need to stay on fire. I am smashing on this erg. I can hear Alvin yanking the handle. I finish and jump up to look for a puke bucket, feeling dizzy. The team is throwing my hands up. I don't know what's happening. I am #1 in the city and #35 in the country for the Junior Men 2K. I am excited to see if I can web search my name and have my score pop up. I also broke my record, testing at 7 minutes for seventeen-year-olds. Alvin didn't rank but proved to himself that he can compete. He hugs me and says next stop spring break training.

Winter flies by and indoor season is almost over. There is no time for hanging out at the mall, watching TV, or chasing girls. Well, Alvin always finds time to chase girls even though he is still with Maria, who has finally learned how to put a sentence together in English.

Pookie G. and Alvin attend church with me on Sundays, and Ken and Winnifred pop up every once in a while. Ken even donated some money to Victory Outreach because he loves their mission and he knows that they get results. Josh has become the little brother of the team, finally opening up about being bullied his whole life and how comedy has helped him. He tells us the popular kids clowned him daily because his clothes weren't name brand. He says that being bullied hurts way more than getting punched in the face. I second that one because being laughed at makes you want to drop out of school, hurt someone, or hurt yourself.

Josh says he listened to cassettes by Redd Foxx, Eddie Murphy, and Richard Pryor. Then he went to school and before someone opened their mouth to talk about him, he would tell a joke. Every day after that, people would ask him to make them laugh. The bullying stopped. We've all gotten close to him since he began to open up, and we always tell him that one day millions of people will laugh at his comedy.

After all of our ups and downs, I finally feel complete as a team. Marc is the best coach that we could ever ask for. When we run, he runs farther. When we do push-ups, he does more. When we have study sessions, he corrects us. When we watch rowing videos, he quizzes us, and when he sees physical results, he puts us on the erg machine and he evaluates us. We call him the Marcanator.

Before I know it, the time is near to go to Philly again for spring break training camp. Marc decides to invite other students so we can have reserves and Coach Jessica will come along with some girls. I need extra cash for the trip so I call my uncle Terry and ask if I can work as a laborer for his construction company. My uncle Terry has been doing well for a year now since he graduated from the Victory Outreach recovery home in California. He was a severe addict, but then he saw my mother change and decided that he needed to go far away and do the same for himself and his kids. When he came back he started a construction business and hired young guys to keep them off the street.

On Saturday I take the train to the South Side and meet my uncle at one of the buildings he is working on. He is one of those old-school uncles who asks all his questions at one time and answers them at the same time.

"Where you been? At school. Where ya momma? At home. How you losing weight? Not eating."

Before I can say anything, he grabs me. "Come on, boy, let me show you what you doing."

My uncle has me hanging drywall with him. While we are working, the owner of the building walks in and says hello. She is an older lady with gray hair. She asks my uncle questions about his life and where he grew up. Turns out they both grew up in the same neighborhood and they start ticking off mutual friends. The woman asks my uncle if he knows the Lattimores and my heart starts pounding.

"Norman or Dennis Lattimore?" I ask her.

"Yes, Norman is my godson."

I feel my heart throb in my chest. "That's my dad."

She gives me a hug and tells me I look just like him. I give her a fake smile, and she says she is going to call him.

"Please, not now."

"Well," she says, "I am going to give you his number."

"You are so nice," I tell her, "but can you just give him mine?"

She gives me a long look and agrees to give him my number. She is excited and says she can't wait to call and talk to him.

I continue working as memories of Norman start coming back. When I would get in trouble as a little kid, my mom would beat me and tell me I was a mistake. When she was on drugs, she would make the same claim and I never understood why.

The first time I met Norman I was nine years old. My mom told me to come to the door because there was someone she wanted me to meet. I walked to the door and saw him and knew it was my dad. He looked at me with a big smile on his face.

"Hey, I am your dad." I looked down at his hand and it was full of quarters.

"I am coming to get you this weekend and we will hang out."

"Okay." I nodded eagerly.

"Okay, son, I will see you then." I said good-bye and he started walking down the stairs. I asked my mom if I could ask him for a dollar. She said yes, so I ran after him and asked him for a dollar. He said he didn't have a dollar bill on him, but would bring me one that weekend. I nodded and walked back up the stairs.

That weekend he came to pick me up for a family Halloween party. My mom didn't buy me a costume, so she covered my face with her red lipstick and sent me on my way. I remember being there and feeling left out because everyone had a costume and no one paid me any attention. He left me with his sister and her son that whole weekend and I had a blast. They were fun and glad to have me. When he picked me up, he took me back to his apartment and introduced me to his mom and dad and his brother, Dennis; they were all hospitable.

After he dropped me off at home, I told my mom that I had a lot of fun and I wanted to go back soon. I called his number every day after that weekend for months. I must have dialed that string of digits over a thousand times. He never answered. That was the last time I saw him. I would daydream in elementary school that he might come pick me up in his red pickup truck with the cab only big enough for me and him. All the kids from class would ask to jump in the back and I always let them.

I snap out of my thoughts and my uncle is looking at me. He knows what I'm going to say.

"What a coward."

My uncle nods. "But you probably wouldn't be the guy you are today."

When I get home I tell my mom what happened at work.

She sits and says, "Arshay, Norman was a friend and a bad alcoholic. One day, we both got really drunk and he kept asking to have sex with me because he said he had a crush on me, but I never liked him like that. After a few more drinks, I told him maybe."

"Oh, no. I can't listen to this."

"Arshay, listen. We slept together once, and I had you. I am happy for that, and you are not a mistake. God wants you here." I tell her that if Norman calls I will talk to him, and she is happy.

"Thank God for alcohol," I mumble sarcastically as I close my door.

The phone rings around 9 p.m. and I know it is him. I pick up the phone and he asks for Arshay.

"Speaking."

"It's your dad," he says, sounding so happy that my attitude suddenly changes. We talk about his godmother and I tell him what I'm up to. We talk about him and his family. He tells me that he got married and moved to Country Club Hills, which is an hour outside the city. Norman asks if I can come to his place for the weekend to hang out. I tell him I can't do a weekend, but I can come for a day. He wants to know why I can't come for a weekend, and a million reasons run through my mind. Instead I say that we should start off slow and get to know each other. He gets frustrated and tells me to hold on.

A few seconds later, his wife gets on the phone. "Arshay, we love you and want you to come and stay just for the weekend." I tell her it's very nice to meet her, but can I please speak to Norman. He gets back on the phone and I tell him again that I would love to come for a day. He tells me he will call me back and we hang up.

I'm not sure if I handled it well. One part of me says a visit should be on my terms, and the other part is saying that I should just go with the flow. I do want to know a lot of things about my family. I want to know our history, if I will go bald, where I get some of my bad habits. I just don't feel right so I decide to call back, and we decide to meet later in the week on the West Side at his sister's place.

I am walking to meet Norman with butterflies in my stomach. I told the guys on the team the story and they all offered to come with me. I didn't take them up on it, but it felt good to know they have my back. Josh told me to ask for child support money. He is good at cheering me up with jokes.

When I turn the corner on South Kedzie Avenue and West Douglas Boulevard I see Norman and his wife on the porch. They both jump up and give me hugs. Looking at him is like looking at me in the future. He has the same rich brown eyes, curly Afro, and chestnut-colored skin. He looks me over, takes a deep breath, and says, "Son."

We head into my aunt's apartment and they show me pictures of my grandparents, cousins, aunts, and uncles. It is surreal. My aunt seems nervous, and I can tell she just wants everything to work out. Norman is very talkative while I am a little bashful. I can't read his wife, as she doesn't say much. I open up for twenty minutes about rowing and they are all agog. Shortly after, we say our good-byes and I tell him to keep in touch. I feel good about seeing him, but still can't get past the neglect. I will leave the ball in his court to reach out.

14

Spring Break

The next week we are off to Philly for spring break. There are seven boys, and seven girls, plus Marc and Coach Jessica. There are two fifteen-passenger vans; the boys ride with Marc and the girls with Coach Jessica. Marc will focus on coaching the guys and getting us ready for the race at Grand Rapids. It's a big race for the high school Midwest teams, and we can't stop talking about it. Coach Jessica will coach the girls she recently recruited. The girls are Ana, Leslie, Zinanta, Antonia, Delilah, Shaquis, and Entantra. We spend the whole time listening to Josh crack jokes about the girls in the other van and us. He is one of the only guys who can make Marc laugh. We crack on Josh because every time Marc drops him off or picks him up at home, his grandmother smacks him across the head for something he said. Marc is terrified of Josh's grandmother and we think she's a little nuts, maybe even packing heat. The old lady never stops yelling. Josh always says if it weren't for his crazy grandmother he wouldn't have any comedy material.

We sleep half of the trip but Josh stays up the whole time. He tells us he doesn't want to miss anything. He is such a good kid. Josh spends all day making people laugh, but I know that when he gets home to the four walls of his room he feels alone, so we make a pact to cover him with brotherly love.

Elliot is sleeping and has his headphones on throughout the trip. A lot of students at school give Elliot shit for being a bit of a nerd. Those are the people that will be reading his books, using his technology, and shopping at his store.

Pookie G. sticks by Alvin on this bus ride. He looks up to him. Alvin feels a need to protect him as he does his family. Pookie G. found his confidence by ordering us around as the coxswain.

Alvin loves these trips. To me, his life has had the most significant turnaround. The team has been counting each day Alvin has gone without a fight. It is literally the funniest thing. Even Marc has got into the joke.

When we finally make it to Philly, Marc pulls into a grocery store to get food before heading to the youth hostel. There is a Latina girl inside the store and Alvin starts singing "My, My, My" by Johnny Gill to her while walking behind her. She can't stop smiling. She stops and tells him he has a nice voice and asks how old he is. He lies and says eighteen, which is how old she looks.

"I'm in town for a week for a race. You should give me a call."

He gives her Marc's cell number and tells her to call him tonight. You can tell Alvin has made quite an impression on her.

We get to the hostel and all the girls complain about the healthy food Marc bought. The guys are fine since healthy eating is a lifestyle to us now. We cheat a couple of times a week but not around Marc. Marc sits us all down to explain the schedule for the week and his phone starts ringing. He picks up the phone and we can hear a muffled voice.

"Can I speak to Alvin?" We all start laughing.

"Who is this?"

"I just met Alvin at the supermarket."

"No, you can't talk to him."

Alvin starts pleading with him but Marc hangs up the phone, his face beet red. He does not play games when it comes to rowing business. The phone rings again and Marc picks it up.

"You can't talk to him," he says and hangs up again.

She keeps calling, so Marc has to turn his phone off.

"Listen up," Marc says, "we are here to work; this is not a vacation."

I can tell he is also frustrated with the girls, because they came out with their hair and nails done and new outfits.

"You are going to work your butts off. We will wake up at five a.m. to run hills and then row. Then we'll go to the university and sit in on some of the classes, eat lunch, and go back to the boathouse to row. Every day, guys, that's the plan."

The girls look like someone just stole their man. I am fine with it; 5 a.m. does seem a little extreme for spring break, but that's the crew culture.

In the morning we are at the boathouse at 5:40 a.m. The girls stick around to stretch with Coach Jessica and Marc tells us to run fifteen minutes out and fifteen minutes back while he checks out the boat. We run past Boathouse Row and along the Schuylkill River for five minutes and then Alvin stops.

"This is insane. It's early and we're on spring break."

Tyromeo, one of the new guys, nods in agreement. "Marc is extreme."

They all sit on a bench and look up at me.

"Arshay, we're training again later today. We are not running ten more minutes down this path."

This is a little insane for spring break, but I want to win.

"We are already doing two a day, Arshay," Pookie G. says.

"Okay, we can talk."

We relax for twenty minutes and then run back down to the boathouse. Marc puts the regular rotation in a four-boat, while Tydon and Tyromeo wait to get on the next round. It's our first time on the water with Marc and he preaches perfection the whole time. We spend a lot of time on one-handed feather drills to perfect our feathering. He also improves our posture, drive, stroke, and finish. Marc has the eye of the tiger and rarely blinks when we are on the water. When we're rowing with Marc, we aren't four individuals, we're one, entirely in sync. We row past the college rowers and Josh is eyeing them down like crazy. "Stop, Josh," Elliot tells him.

"Okay, guys, every time we pass the college rowers we are going to haul ass."

"Yeah nigga, that's what I am talking about!" Alvin yells.

Coach Marc continues to motivate us down the course, smiling like we just learned how to ride a bike.

"Guys, now you are a crew," Marc says to us as we take it back to the dock.

I think we've done so well because we've spent hours and hours on the erg machine working on our technique. The college teams at UPenn praise us for how strong we are and can't believe we are high school students. They tell us to perfect our technique and we will be monsters.

There are two days left of training before we go home and so far spring break has been all blood, sweat, and tears. These two-a-days got me ready to talk Loyola St. Ignatius into an unofficial race. As Marc said, we've worked our butts off. We run down the path and lie on the bench as usual, but we are so tired that we fall asleep. I wake up to Alvin.

"Here comes Marc!"

I look up and see him running toward us in his purple Northwestern jacket. I don't know how long we were asleep, but we jump up and start running toward this bridge. Marc is screaming something at us but we keep running as if nothing happened. Marc is on our tail until we get back to the boathouse. I know we're about to catch hell.

We walk into the locker room and he throws his clipboard against the locker and yells from the top of his lungs, "Did I catch you guys *sleeping*? Did you guys do this every day?"

We are all silent.

"Again, did you do this every day?"

Quietly, I say, "Yes."

"I trusted you!" he screams. I put my head down. He is so angry.

"I give you guys all I have and you don't give it back in return. You know what they're saying about you? You're a joke, you are *just* athletic, that you don't belong here. I thought everyone was wrong. You guys almost fooled me."

We don't say a word; we are so disappointed in ourselves. Marc stops screaming and tells us that we have rights. "The right to be here, the right to win, and the right to be rowers. You just don't know it." He picks up his clipboard and walks out of the locker room.

"We gonna wear the spandex or what?" Josh jokes, trying to cut the tension.

I jump up and walk into the workout room. I reach into my gym bag and grab a CD, put it on the radio, and sit on the erg machine and row. All the guys come in; Alvin sits next to me and the others sit to my right, and we row. Tydon is screaming as he rows. We just let it all out. This machine allows us to let go of our anger, our past, our disappointments, and our sorrows.

Tupac's "Dear Mama" starts playing, and I have a moment. We have a moment. We stop rowing and begin to rap along to the song.

It means something to all of us. No matter what inner city you are from in America, when it comes on you stop what you're doing and you rap along with Tupac. It is our story in a song.

Marc walks in and stares at us. He turns the music off.

"Grand Rapids, Michigan."

We look at him with fire in our eyes.

"We won't let you down, Coach."

I know that this is the beginning of a new era for us. Nothing has to be said, this is the end of us playing games. We have the eye of the tiger.

15

Chasing Gold

The sun is shining down on us as we recline in the boat, enjoying the breeze. Our new ritual is to lean back and enjoy the water after a hard day of practice. The same water that we used to fear has become our place of refuge. We don't just live to row but row to live. It's been over a month since Philly and we've been breaking our backs to get ready for the big race in Michigan. The guys don't want to be at home, school, or on the West Side. The want to be here at the boathouse.

Pookie G., Alvin, Elliot, Josh, and I continue to grow stronger as a team.

Marc finally trusts us. Every time we sprint, do push-ups, or wall-sits, I challenge Marc, but to no avail. He is really good. I've become competitive and brutally hard on myself. People always tell me that I'm young and should enjoy being a teenager, but to me it's only temporary fun. Being a teenager is all about fake friends, being broke, and a constant battle for popularity.

While I lean back in the boat, I think about Ken's first speech in the gym when he told us that if we went on this journey with him, we would succeed. I think having a million dollars would be fantastic, and being on TV or the radio would be cool, but giving a kid your word and watching them change must do something on the inside that's better than what those other things can do for you on the outside.

"Hey, guys, look up." Pookie G. interrupts my daydream.

A group of black people on the bridge are giving us fist pumps and yelling "Go get it!" We give them fist pumps back. We figure that they looked down and saw all the white teams and we're the only black guys so they want to show us some love. We get that all the time at the lagoon.

Pookie G. asks us, "What's the most embarrassing thing that ever happened to you guys?" We start laughing.

"You don't even want to know." Alvin shakes his head.

"Do tell," I say, curious.

"When I was in sixth grade, this boy was talking trash and I knew I could beat him up. I told everyone in school to watch me knock this kid out at lunch. So, when I got to lunch all the girls and boys were waiting for me to do it. I got up and walked toward him while everyone was looking, and got close enough to hit him. Before I could, he pulled out a Butterfinger candy bar and whacked me across the forehead and I passed out."

We start cracking up, and Alvin tells us that when he opened his eyes everyone was laughing, saying he got knocked out by a Butterfinger.

"I know that commercial, 'Nobody better lay a finger on my Butterfinger,'" I tell him, laughing. "What about you, Josh?"

Josh thinks about it for a second. "I was in second grade, I think. Before class started, I was outside and my friend dared me to go and do the moonwalk in front of the girls. So I go over and do it, and I just kept going. It was easy because it was raining a little, but I slipped in the mud and landed on my face and everyone started laughing. My older cousin just turned around and acted like he didn't know me."

Everyone makes a face.

"Ooh."

"Ouch."

"Damn."

"That one is rough," I tell him. "What about you, Pookie G.?"

"I can't think of one. You go first and come back to me."

"Okay, mine was in third grade. This kid, Rashad, had all the cute girls. I mean, they all liked him. I was confused because he had so many scars on his face and it always glowed. So I went to my little baby cousin Jen Jen's place one day and started a fight with her, because I knew she would scratch my face up. She scratched me up pretty bad, and my mom was pissed.

"The next morning I got up for school and put a handful of Vaseline on my scarred face to look like Rashad. I walked into the classroom and my teacher took one look at me and said, 'Boy, if you don't wash that Vaseline off your face.' All the girls were pointing and laughing. I guess he was just good looking."

All the guys laugh. "Don't worry, that story is going to get you a fine chick one day," Josh assures me.

St. Ignatius Loyola rolls up next to our boat and we know what they are thinking. This wakes Josh up real fast. Elliot rolls up his shirt sleeve to show his guns, and Pookie G. yells, "Five hundred meters!"

"Let's get alignment," the St. Ignatius coxswain says.

We have been waiting for this. I haven't lost a competition in a while.

"Bury your blades," Pookie G. tells us.

I know we shouldn't be doing this. Marc would snap. *But fuck it.*

"Row."

We take off, and their boat is right next to us.

"Okay, guys, full pressure!" Pookie screams.

We both are pushing it down the lagoon. I am looking at the John Hancock Building as we go. Their boat is super steady and their blades are not even touching the water.

"Okay, on my momma, y'all better move this damn boat."

The boat jumps as I turn up like never. We hit the lead and our boat moonwalks the water like Michael Jackson in his prime.

"Let it run."

We smoke them. Alvin screams, "Yeah!"

They smile and give head nods of respect and we wave and smile back in a huff.

We dock and put the boat away excited because we are two weeks away from the biggest race of our lives in Grand Rapids, Michigan. We've been fighting hard all year, and I think we might actually have a chance to win. I haven't seen anyone that can move the boat the way we do at our practice site. We've finally earned the one thing that we were searching for: respect. Respect from our coaches, family, friends, the school, the football team, and now St. Ignatius Loyola. It was lonely for us without that respect in the early days of rowing. Marc has worked hard to teach us to respect ourselves, our bodies, our time, our boat, our competitors, our teammates, and the crew culture. When we finally figured that out, the world overflowed with an abundance of respect right into our laps. Manley Crew is ready to make a big impact.

Before we go home Marc tells us we are rowing like champs.

"You guys have earned that title. We're going to Northwestern and Buffalo Joe's this weekend." We get super excited and Alvin tells Pookie G. he may win coxswain of the year for calling us every name in the book.

"The angry coxswain," I tell him.

"Whatever it takes to get the job done," Pookie G. says with a smile.

The next morning, I'm walking down the hallway at school when Mrs. Dunn, the business school teacher, asks me if I'm interested in becoming the class treasurer.

"Sure, no problem."

"Amazing! Come during lunch period, we have pizza!"

"I can eat."

I am overcommitting, I think, but this is all great for college admissions. So, yes has been my favorite word.

At lunch, I head down to Mrs. Dunn's room for our class meeting. When I walk into the classroom, everyone is sitting at a round table. There is one seat left open, and it is right across from Grace. I sit, on guard. At the table are Derrick, Grace, and a few others. Grace is the vice president. I haven't talked to Grace in months, and it feels strange to be sitting here not looking at her. I keep my face fixed on Mrs. Dunn. I can feel Grace's energy trying to get me to acknowledge her, but I'm sure she feels from my energy that I am dying to leave the room. I am definitely strong enough to sit in the same room as her, I just don't want to.

Mrs. Dunn talks about the roles and responsibilities that we have in the positions we hold, but all I can think about is the upcoming race. I've learned to block things out of my head and guard my heart the same way I guard my teammates. I haven't talked to my dad since seeing him, and it hurts a lot less than last time. I've learned to count my blessings, and there are always more positives than negatives. I've learned how to strengthen myself.

"Arshay, what do you think?" I look up and realize she's asking me a question and I have no idea what she is talking about.

"Um . . . I have a tight schedule, but wherever there is a need I'm happy to help," I tell her, hoping it has anything to do with her question.

"Awesome."

The meeting goes on for ten more minutes, and then we're dismissed. I pack up slowly so I don't have to walk out with Grace, but I notice she is moving slow, too. I speed up and rush to the door and somehow she is right there. I drop my pride and return her look.

"Hey, you," I say, smiling. I feel her happiness.

"I've missed you, Arshay."

"Sorry for being distant."

"It's okay, you're right here."

She smells like maple and I start to get flooded with memories. I feel dizzy. Her words are smooth and she is so beautiful. I know she wants to share her frustrations and everything she's going through, but she doesn't. Derrick walks out of the classroom and passes us and she quietly loses herself for that second. I see it in her eyes.

It hurts, but I let go of the possibility of "someday" because no one gets out of the friend zone unless all other options are completely gone.

"Okay then, my friend, I have to go, but we are going to hang, Big Head."

"Are you going to the school roller skating trip?" she asks.

"I may, but see you soon."

We both walk off in the same direction without saying a word; I head downstairs and she heads upstairs. I feel mostly fine. Some people say the heart does what it wants and you can't control it. I think it's what you feed the heart. For the first time, I was able to stand next to her and not be totally awestruck. I decide I will keep that poem until the last day of school.

Saturday morning is beautiful as we head to Northwestern University in Evanston. Alvin, Josh, Pookie G., Elliot, and I are pumped. It is just a short ride from the city. Once we start seeing people wearing purple everywhere we know we are there. The buildings are imposing gray monoliths and the campus is spotless, situated on beautiful Lake Michigan with student access to the beach.

"This is a good school to come to for rowing," Marc tells us, "and all you guys should think about filling out an application."

"Maybe I will," Josh says, looking around.

We head to the athletic facility and can tell that the guys there are serious about working out. Everyone is in amazing shape. We see where Marc gets his work ethic from. We stay in the athletic facility for an hour and watch the guys train, stealing workout methods from the strength and conditioning coach in the cardio room. Marc walks us around the entire campus and gives us the history of each building. We are constantly learning. We lie out on the grass and crack jokes on each other. Seems like college life is everything *A Different World* cracked it up to be. We walk over to Buffalo Joe's and I tell Marc these better be the best wings we've ever had.

"Get the jalapeño wings. They're the best if you like spicy."

We take his advice and tears are flowing from how spicy they are. He wins. I have never tasted a better wing.

"Yeah, Arshay," Josh says, "that's because the only wings you've had is chicken they sell in the hood: Harold's, Leon's, or Uncle Remus's."

"Exactly," I tell him.

This is our first cheat meal with Marc and everyone is so relaxed. He is a perfectionist and he's taught us to aim for precision in everything we do; we've taught him to relax and live a little. We love Marc and he loves us, and the family continues to grow. Ken and Victory Outreach have taught me to have vision and to see where I want to be and what to do to get there. I feel like even if we stop now, we've accomplished what Ken wanted from us. We succeeded the moment we stepped in the boat for the first time. As the captain, my vision is for the guys to know that we're not just a team, we're a movement. As the first black men in this position, we can make history and be heroes. I don't want people to look at us and see students, or rowers, or our skin color. I want them to see hope.

To our parents, we may be a rowing team. To our competition, we may be a joke. But in reality, we are a force. Our school is our base and we need to protect it like soldiers. If there is a fight, we should break it up, no questions asked. If there is a fire drill, we should help, no questions asked. If our coaches ask us to run a mile, we should run two, no questions asked. The person to our left or our right is not just a teammate, he's a brother.

A captain is not chosen just for ability, or talent, or strength, but for their leadership. Captains should be the first to set foot in the boathouse and the last to leave, not the coaches. A captain understands that every push-up, sit-up, diet, sprain, scar, lecture, and sprint is not a punishment but a way of life and a state of mind.

I look around at my teammates: some of their mothers are drug addicts, their fathers are nowhere to be found, brothers are in gangs, sisters are having babies, uncles are in jail, friends are dying, and refrigerators are empty. But we are a beacon of light. We aren't making the same impact that the Tuskegee Airmen did, or winning like the University of Texas at El Paso basketball team has, or going to the Olympics like the Jamaican bobsled team, but we are making a big difference to our families and those who come in contact with us. We mean the world to them. We went into this thinking we would change the sport of rowing like Jackie Robinson did baseball, but the sport of crew has changed us. We are becoming Dr. King's vision of a beloved community.

At the end of the school year there's always a big skating party for Manley. The music is banging, the room is dark, and some of the best skaters in Chicago are out to skate. We are at Rainbo Roller Center on Clark Street. Manley always treats the students to an outing toward the end of the school year. Rainbo scares me at times because I've heard stories of people getting robbed, stabbed, or shot after skate nights. There are more than three hundred students present and we are ending a good year.

I don't skate much. I want to lay low because it's race week and I'm not much of a skater. I'm sitting at a table in the dining area when someone creeps up behind me and puts me in a choke hold. I tap out right away because I know it's Preston. I know his choke hold.

"Sup, sweet pea?" He hates that name. It was given to him by Tara, the girl he chased for years and is still chasing.

"What I tell you about calling me that," he says, trying to put me back into a choke hold.

"Don't shoot."

He laughs and gives me a bro hug. I don't see Preston as much anymore because one month he will be at school and the next month he doesn't show up.

"Coop, I just want to say I'm proud of you, my dude. I should have stuck with crew but I got caught up in other interests."

"Remember when we were in, like, sixth grade, and the older guys would drive past and you wanted to pretend play it was our car?"

"Yeah." Preston laughs. "That was fun."

"Then we started seeing those same guys from the hood rocking diamond earrings, so we would say, 'Those are my earrings.'" He laughs as we reminisce.

"So we waited until nighttime to find a firefly and then took the bulbs out and put 'em in our ear to pretend our diamonds were better."

"Yeah, that was like the best three seconds ever."

"I valued those cars and diamonds. I saw the way life has ended up for those guys, and my values changed."

"That's why I said I'm proud of you, my dude." He looks at the carpet, unsure of how to continue. "I'm not gonna lie. I sell drugs, and my mom is out there so bad, Coop. She's on the stuff. She took my money jar and broke it in the street and took money."

"Preston . . . I'm so sorry. Let me know what I can do. There *is* Victory Outreach."

"I know," he says, getting up. "I'm about to grab some skates."

"Sweet pea," I say, and he turns back around. "There is always a seat for you on that boat."

"I'll be back, Coop."

When I get home, my mom is reading. She's always reading. Sometimes I think she might be too extreme. She nearly passed out a few months ago because she fasted for six days, drinking only water. I have seen the results of her dedication, because Shaundell is still in the Victory Outreach home in Rockford. My younger brother Isaac, on the other hand, is a different story. My mom sent him to the home on the weekends to learn some discipline and he hit the director in the back of the head with a brush, so they sent him back. Isaac is my responsibility, my little brother.

My mom tells me, "You fight for your kids, and you forgive them, and you pray. Then you wake up the next morning and you fight for them again, be an example, forgive them again and you pray."

All I know is that we are not where we used to be. We have dinner together, there are no zombies in our hallway, and we have reasons to smile when we wake up and go to sleep. If my family can change, so can everyone else's.

One night on an episode of *A Different World*, Dwayne Wayne tells a story about fleas living in a jar, constantly jumping and banging their heads on the lid. One day, the lid is removed and the fleas refuse to jump out into the unknown, essentially putting the lid on themselves. I feel like in my community, people put limits on themselves and their neighbors. I refuse to live that way. I want to be open to any good idea from anyone with heart. I know people are going to judge me, but like my friend Jerome always says, "The only thing worse than people talking about you is when no one is talking about you."

It's early and Marc just scooped me up in his Jeep, and the guys are already in the car. I see that Josh is reading *Animal Farm*.

"What, Josh, no more Game Boy?" I ask.

"Gotta feed the brain, homie."

It's a quiet ride to the Pilsen neighborhood. We used to joke nonstop, but one of the biggest lessons we have learned as a team is that there is a time and place. We pull up to this vacant area and see the St. Ignatius rowing team and a lot more people.

"So what are we doing again?" Alvin asks.

"A few rowing clubs are moving from the lagoon to the Chicago River to row. There's way more space here, so we are going to volunteer and help build a dock, boat racks, put up a fence, trim the grass, and clean the area."

"For free?" Josh asks.

"Yes," Marc says, laughing.

"Y'all people got free employment out of us for 200 years; enough is enough," Josh says jokingly. We all crack up.

"Are we going to be rowing here?"

"Yes, we will."

I get out of the car and walk over to check out the river and it is in rough shape. There are condoms, tree branches, and all kinds of trash flying by.

"You think there are dead bodies in there?"

I turn, and it's the guys from the St. Ignatius Loyola team talking to me. I see Josh and the guys walk over fast as if they thought I was about to get jumped. So I fake laugh, hoping the guys see my face and recognize that it's all good.

"Arshay," I say, reaching out my hand for a shake. They all start introducing themselves, and my guys come and shake hands with them. It's unreal that for two years we haven't spoken unless it was shit-talking.

"I remember your first day on the boat," one of the guys tells Josh.

"Do you remember that race last week at the lagoon?" Everyone starts laughing. Some girls from the University of Chicago crew team walk past, and all the guys from both teams are gawking. The folks in charge break us all into different groups to work. Music is blasting; everyone is getting their hands dirty, and Josh is running around, making everyone crack up and also trying to set Marc up with the college rowers. I cannot wait for this site to finish so I can say, we did this!

I didn't think we could get along with people who didn't look like us but rowing changed that for me. Crew changed our mindset, lifestyle, work ethic, and, as Elliot says, "our bodies." This experience was just never just about rowing. It was about bridging the water. When I think about Harriet Tubman, I don't think about her career as a union spy, but I think of freedom. When I hear the name Dr. King, I don't imagine an educated pastor, but I picture hope. When Gandhi is spoken of, I think of peace and not his occupation as an attorney. When you represent something larger than yourself and your career, real change happens. So when we step out into that boat in Grand Rapids, I don't want people to see a crew team but young men who rowed against the current of life and survived.

WELCOME TO MICHIGAN!

I see that sign and nerves instantly shoot down my body. It's April of 1999 and today is the biggest race we've ever been in. I feel like it's our make-or-break moment. We are focused, nervous, strong, lean, prepared, and confident. I can tell we have been brainwashed by rowing because we went from talking dirty on road trips to talking about split times, oar blades, and what boathouse has nice decks. After thinking about the stuff we used to think and say, I believe a brainwashing was necessary.

We park in front of a huge gymnasium and hop out of the van to stretch. High school rowers are everywhere. They all have sleeping bags in their hands because all two hundred students are camping out in the gym overnight. Josh gets out of the van and whistles at all the white girls.

"The land of milk and honey."

"Is that yours or Pryor's?" I ask him, laughing.

"Mine."

We walk into the gym and it's filled with laughter and people having a good time. Josh insists that even I could have fun here. He stays on my case about relaxing and having fun, and even calls me "Mini-Marc." I do have fun at times, but I've also never gotten over running into a brick wall, and the look on everyone's faces when we did.

We sit in a circle and Marc gives us our shorts. They are cotton throwback shorts, with *Manley* written in red on the bottom. I am happy with them. Josh makes a comment about the shorts being Daisy Dukes and we laugh, but I look at them and feel proud to be a Manley Wildcat. I feel like we could have been amazing if we'd had the school supporting us the whole time, but it's fine. We are right where we need to be.

We people watch for an hour or so and then Marc tells us to hit the showers. When we walk into the shower room, its community style and everyone is naked. We agree that is not happening for us, so we shower in our shorts and then head to bed.

At 5 a.m., Marc wakes me up. I look around and everybody is still sleeping. He tells us it's time to run, so the five of us start running and sprinting outside.

Afterward, he says, "While everyone is sleeping, you're working. You guys are the most creative, talented, strongest, funniest guys I know. Words can't express how proud I am of you."

A few hours later, we're at the regatta, watching early races. As always, we're the only black people there and we have mixed emotions about it. Some of the guys are focused and don't get bothered anymore; the others say it still bothers them because there should be more of us here racing. A tall man with caramel skin and a long, wavy ponytail approaches. He looks Indian or mixed. He shakes Marc's hand and stares at us.

"I consider this a pleasure to meet you all. My name is Coach Tim Fields. I'm coaching one of the races here."

We say hello but he keeps staring at us, intrigued. He pulls Marc aside to ask how he can get involved.

"That's weird," Alvin whispers.

"Yeah, that's how I looked when I got new G. I. Joes."

Marc tells us it's time to race and my stomach drops. We head over to get our boat and Pookie G. walks us out to the water, loud and clear for everyone to hear. People stare, as usual. We walk out like a drill team, focused and walking in sync. We don't look anywhere but forward. We are all chiseled, dark, and handsome. Our strong presence tells everyone we are here to win. I know, without a shadow of a doubt, it is our time. We've given up everything this year for today. It is our moment.

Pookie G. yells "Way enough" right before we get to the dock, so we wait to get on the water. We drop our hands with the boat resting on our shoulders. It hurts like hell but looks incredible.

I don't care if you're an Olympian, a Harvard rower, or test at four minutes in a 2,000-meter piece—there are no rowers I would rather row with than these guys. None of us had ever said as much as hello to each other in the halls before rowing, but now we are brothers. Basketball, football, and baseball couldn't have done what rowing has done to this group. It has taken nonathletic, nerdy, small, broken, and uncool kids and made them a family. Every time we get into the water, we are adding something to it that rowing has never seen before.

Each one of us adds our different flavor: Alvin, the gangsta with the big heart; Josh, the funny man with a famous stare down that distracts all the other rowers. Elliot is the guy with the slick box haircut who pushes one sleeve up and one down on his shirt. And, of course, our coxswain, Pookie G., singing and rapping and calling us every curse word in the Book of Ebonics.

We may be a little rough around the edges, but we'll race with a purpose far greater than who might win.

A symbol for what can be possible when unlikely gang rivals manage to come together as one. When I look at them, it's the most beautiful thing I've ever seen.

We get in the boat, and families are everywhere screaming, ringing bells, blowing whistles, taking photos, and holding up signs. On one side of the water I see tents and vendors and on the other parents and spectators. This feels so surreal. It's like the Super Bowl of junior rowing. St. Ignatius Loyola is on the water, as well as St. Mary, Ann Arbor, Culver, and many other Midwest schools.

Josh tells us that after this win we are going to run in the hood with this boat on our shoulders to make a statement. All the boats are lined up and I count six in total. It is a 1,500-meter race. As we slide up to the catch, I bury my blade; my hands are shaking, my heart is racing, my neck hairs are standing up, and I am taking fewer breaths. I close my eyes and wait to hear his voice. I start thinking about Preston, Malcolm, Mom, Shaundell, Ken, Coach Victor, and all those who have been on this journey. I open my eyes and accept the moment and think to myself the affluent world of crew is about to get rocked.

"We got alignment. *Row!*"

We take off so fast the boat hops on the water. After every stroke, Pookie G. howls. We are pushing hard, and for the first time we are in the lead. Screams and chants are coming at us from every direction. Sweaty palms, hot sun, painful strokes—it doesn't matter. We row with everything we have.

There is a boat on our left that is close, and now just passes us.

"Okay, Wildcats, power ten in two!" Pookie G. yells, "One. Two. Now get it!"

We begin to smash. We are owning it in seconds. We gain speed and right to this boat. I feel like we're flying. "Yeah, we are moving, go after it!" Pookie G. is yelling. This feels so electric and the crowd is amazing. Everything is hurting but I'm digging deep.

There are three boats completely behind us. I look to my left and Marc is screaming and running toward the finish line, pumping his fist. I have never seen him so happy. I look to the right and I see 400 meters left. I take a look at the other boats and lose focus for just a heartbeat. My oar drops in the water a half second too late and it swings toward me as I lose control. The oar flies up and slaps me right below my neck.

I fall backward and the oar sails behind me. Marc stops and screams. He instantly turns bright red.

I caught a crab. Alvin yells, "Stop rowing! Arshay, get your oar."

Pookie G. screams, "Keep rowing! Arshay, get your oar," as he slaps the water with his hands.

The boat to our left passes us and another one is quickly approaching. I grab the oar and pull it in front of me and start trying to row. It is hard to get back in sync. The second boat passes us. Pookie G. is yelling but I hear nothing, I just row as hard as I can. We catch up to the second boat, but I see we are too late—they cross the finish line ahead of us. We finish third.

I drop my body forward onto my lap and cry. I haven't cried in years. When sweat meets tears, it's been a fight. Alvin leans forward and puts his hand on my shoulder. I can't get Marc's face out of my head. I try so hard with everything I have to be perfect, too hard. I am the leader and I've let everyone down. I failed. I took my eyes off what was ahead of me to see what was behind me, and I am paying for it. Not just me, but my entire team. My actions caused others to fail.

In this moment, with my face in my lap and my heart in my stomach, I can hear my teammates saying thank you. I look up and the teams that have passed the finish line are giving us head nods and thumbs-ups. They are all showing us the utmost respect. There is still one team that hasn't made it past the finish line yet, so we wait and clap for them when they do. While I'm sitting on the boat, I look over at Marc's face. He doesn't show any signs of disappointment, but I know he is. Any coach would be. The only thing I do see on his face is pride. He's never seen anything like this in all his years of rowing. We're a group of black kids from the turbulent West Side of Chicago, surrounded by a group of Midwestern white kids all sharing praise and respect in the middle of a lake. We are all honored to be a part of this, and rowing has helped us achieve Ken's vision for our lives. He once said win or lose, rowing is the tool you use to fix things. Now I understand that. When I was angry, the erg helped;

when I needed peace, the water helped; when I needed discipline, the sport helped. Although I feel bad and unworthy of anything right now, I can't help but think a couple years ago some of us were basically the rejects and outcasts of our communities, but now we are considered the solution. We know who we are.

Beyond winning or losing, past the sound of the start and the cheer of the crowd.

The history we make today is simple: that we survived. I survived my past.

In crew you move ahead by looking in the opposite direction. I learned that it's okay to look back, as long as you keep moving forward.

Epilogue

That was the last time we rowed together as a team. We remained best friends, but we had big dreams we wanted to accomplish individually. Marc moved east to become a college rowing coach, and Tim Fields—who we met in Michigan—took over the program. He turned it into the Chicago Youth Rowing Club, focusing on many public schools. Some of us helped coach.

Alvin credits the entrepreneurship for activating his business mindset. He started a moving business and hired young people from the community who couldn't find a job or wanted to pay for graduation or prom.

Elliot became a full-time chef at the same Marriott where Ken helped him get a job. He started making music and sells it as an entrepreneur.

Pookie G. went to community college and got a job working for UnitedHealthcare. He still goes and helps cox for the master rowing team.

Preston went to jail for a couple of years for selling drugs and got out and started a club promoting business called Lavish Life. He also got his barber license, became one of the best stylists in the city, and won trophies. He gives his time at churches cutting community kids' hair for free.

Preston's mom, Michelle, became very devoted to her church and is a neighborhood mom to her community.

Malcolm moved to Ohio to stay out of trouble and worked for his brother's trucking company until he started his own. He also invests in other local companies.

Coach Jessica became a full-time science teacher at Manley.

Ken and Jeni moved to New York and had four kids. They got a divorce, which broke my heart. I am still so close to them and the kids.

My mom remarried and started running the Victory Outreach Women's Home that she entered many years ago. She changes lives daily and because of that her family is better.

My brothers and sister all had families and are the best parents I know. We remain a praying family.

Ike later went into recovery, remarried, and still lives on the West Side.

Josh was shot and killed a few years after the Grand Rapids race. People say it was a case of being at the wrong place at the wrong time. Friends mourned him and said it was the saddest funeral they'd ever attended. Josh was our medicine; he made us all feel better. He knew exactly what to do and say to fix a situation better than any of us could. I will always love him for that. He taught us that anything and everything can be fixed with laughter. He was so young. I will never understand how a man can kill another man, and then wake up the next morning and go about his day.

I questioned myself, wondering what would've happened if I hadn't followed my personal dreams. If I'd forced us to row in college together, would he still be alive? He was supposed to be the next Chris Rock, but my city is violent. I love my city, it made me who I am. But I cannot accept the violence. What if the local police officers, gang members, aldermen, clergy, firemen, doctors, school principals, basketball teams, grocery-store owners, prosecutors, and community all got together weekly to barbecue, play games, watch sports on an outside projector, play cards, attend Sunday services, teach their trades, build a park, speak, shake hands, learn names, mentor, educate, swap books, give jobs, and trust like our rowing team did. What would the community look like?

When you walk into the doors of City Year AmeriCorps, they tell you a story titled "The Star Thrower" by Loren C. Eiseley. When Ken questions if he really made a difference in our lives, I remind him of the story.

Once, there was a boy walking along a beach. There had just been a storm, and starfish had been scattered along the sands. The boy knew the fish would die, so he began to fling the fish to the sea. But every time he threw a starfish, another would wash ashore. An old man happened along and saw what the child was doing. He called out, "Boy, what are you doing?" "Saving the starfish!" replied the boy. "But your attempts are useless, child! Every time you save one, another one returns, often the same one! You can't save them all, so why bother trying? Why does it matter anyway?" called the old man. The boy thought about this for a while, a starfish in his hand; he answered, "Well, it matters to this one." And then he flung the starfish into the welcoming sea.

I can never thank Ken enough for throwing me into the water because the sport of crew changed my life.

After high school, I took a year and dedicated my life to full service at AmeriCorps working with young children in my community. I then kicked off my career of being a chef by attending Le Cordon Bleu College of Culinary Arts in Chicago and taking extra classes in Le Cordon Bleu London.

Le Cordon Bleu gave me an incredible start and allowed me to see the world as a young chef. First, working at the critically acclaimed restaurant Blackbird, and then moving on to fulfill my dream job as a chef for the famous World Wrestling Entertainment (WWE). After years of experience, I became a personal chef for movie sets, professional athletes, and private events. I then began reflecting on what's next for me and started a young chef program teaching public school kids the career path in the field of cooking in hospitality. The program consisted of learning different cuisines, cooking techniques, nutrition, kitchen safety, proper food handling, knife skills, food meditation, and hospitality.

While working with these young chefs, a recurring question arose. How do I become successful in a community where very few dreams survive? This question sparked my passion for writing about overcoming my childhood hardship, so I began working on my very first book, *Suga Water*. This process heavily inspired my love for the sport of rowing once again. Soon after, I founded the only New York City public school rowing team at East Side Community School for black and Latino students. The model and success of the program made me a highly sought-after motivational speaker and consultant for many rowing programs around the country. I worked alongside coaches to help start rowing programs in Stockton, Minneapolis, Rochester, Seattle, Baltimore, Dallas, Indiana, Chicago, Oakland, Kingston, and New York. On this journey, I recruited and sent kids of color to row in Germany and Spain and at Stanford, Williams, Drexel, and other universities.

Since self-publishing *Suga Water* in 2015, my audience has included corporate organizations, universities, churches, juvenile centers, youth rallies, Stop the Violence marches, recovery homes, and more than 200 charter and public schools. I have won the Benjamin Franklin Award for best inspiration memoir, the Buoy Award for my service in the sport of rowing in New York City, and the USRowing Golden Oars Anita DeFrantz Award for achieving measurable success in expanding diversity opportunities in the sport of rowing. I now sit on the USRowing strategic planning committee for diversity and inclusion while working at Row New York, the largest and most diverse rowing program in the country. I am also working closely with head coaches at universities to diversify the sport and prepare nontraditional rowers for the next few Olympics to come.

Our story is now a documentary titled *A Most Beautiful Thing* directed by Mary Mazzio.

Acknowledgments

I would like to express my gratitude to the many people who saw me through this book. To all of those who provided support, kept pushing me, and believed in my storytelling.

I want to thank Stephanie Cabot, for being the best agent anyone can ask for. I am deeply grateful to the entire Flatiron Books team, especially my publicist, Chris Smith, and my copy editor, Lisa Davis, for working so hard to bring this story to life.

Thank you to my editor, Bryn Clark, for her belief in this project, her patience, and her hard work. A special thanks to Mary Mazzio, the amazing woman who connected me to my agent and made this book a film. Thank you to Clayton Hauck, for the amazing photo.

I must also thank my mother, brothers, sister, the Alpart/Bonjean family, and the Coopers for allowing this story to be told. Huge thanks to the Manley coaches, staff, Alvin, Preston, Malcolm, Pookie G., and other teammates who are all heroes in this story.

A number of dear friends walked this journey alongside me and have given much more than I can ask. A heartfelt thanks goes to Ken Alpart, Rebecca Wheelock, David Banks, Pat Tirone, Amanda Kraus, my Row New York family, Dara Beevas, Richard Butler, Uriah Hall, Mio Pantoja, Denise Aquino, Savi Goodman, Mike Teti, Josh Carlson, Mark Federman,

Paula Miltenberger, Tim Fields, Marc Mandel, the Pocock Foundation family, Margaret Cordi, and Anita Defrantz.

I would like to thank Michael Meacham, who was there when this idea was birthed, for his nonstop help. Without the legal and generous help of Jennifer Bonjean and Derek Dessler, I'm not sure if this book would have happened. I am eternally grateful to my wife, Stacy Bagaloo, who was by my side from beginning to end. You are my motivation and my rock. Thank you, Sasha, my precious daughter who will continue this legacy.

Last but not least, I would like to thank God, and I ask for forgiveness of all those who have been with me over the course of the years whose names I have failed to mention.

About the Author

ARSHAY COOPER is a rower, author, motivational speaker, and volunteer for numerous community outreach organizations. He works with nonprofits focusing on opening the boathouse doors to everyone, and he was the recipient of a 2017 USRowing Golden Oars Award. He lives in Brooklyn with his family.